# RECIPES
## FOR
# MURDER

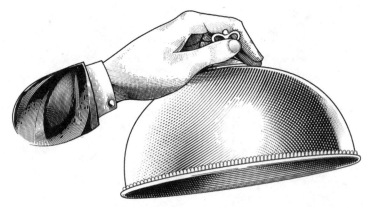

# RECIPES
## FOR
# MURDER

### 66 DISHES THAT
### CELEBRATE THE MYSTERIES
### OF AGATHA CHRISTIE

## KAREN PIERCE

**Countryman Press**

*An Imprint of W. W. Norton & Company*
*Celebrating a Century of Independent Publishing*

To my sister, Sandi

Page ii: iStockPhoto.com / Man_Half-tube; pages 4, 10: iStockPhoto.com / CSA Images; pages 7, 46, 121: iStockPhoto.com / pleshko74; pages 8, 15, 29, 32, 110, 143, 154: iStockPhoto.com / ilbusca; page 10: iStockPhoto.com / Andrew Makarenko; page 13: iStockPhoto.com / Yuliya Derbisheva; pages 18, 39, 108: iStockPhoto.com / NSA Digital Archive; pages 20, 125: iStockPhoto.com / ivan-96; pages 21, 35, 132, 139: iStockPhoto.com / DiViArt; page 27: iStockPhoto.com / Tetiana Lazunova; page 37: iStockPhoto.com / Anton Tokarev; pages 43, 160: iStockPhoto.com / Volodymyr Kryshtal; page 45: iStockPhoto.com / seamartini; pages 49, 63, 74, 116, 147: iStockPhoto.com / Epine_art; page 50: iStockPhoto.com / Maksim Prasolenko; page 53: iStockPhoto.com / GeorgePeters; page 55: iStockPhoto.com / SpicyTruffel; pages 56, 72: iStockPhoto.com / channarongsds; page 58: iStockPhoto.com / Vladayoung; page 61: iStockPhoto.com / ChrisGorgio; pages 68, 144: iStock-Photo.com / THEPALMER; page 70: iStockPhoto.com / antiqueimgnet; pages 76, 82, 84, 86, 97, 123, 141, 152: iStockPhoto.com / Alhontess; pages 77, 103: iStockPhoto.com / Stocknick; page 80: iStockPhoto.com / maystra; page 89: iStockPhoto.com / Mellok; page 90 (stag); iStockPhoto.com / in8finity; page 90 (frame): iStockPhoto.com / PaulFleet; page 93: iStockPhoto.com / Thomas Faull; page 100: iStockPhoto.com / clu; page 113: iStockPhoto.com / Macrovector; pages 117, 134: iStock Photo.com / Arkadivna; page 130: iStockPhoto.com / Ihor Potysiev; page 135: iStockPhoto.com / Serhii Mudruk; page 155: iStockPhoto.com / Mariia Diduk; page 158: iStockPhoto.com / Real Vector; page 162: iStockPhoto.com / suricoma; all decorative borders throughout: iStockPhoto.com / Fourleaflover; all flourishes throughout: iStockPhoto.com / mashakotcur

For information about permission to reproduce selections from this book, write to
Permissions, Countryman Press, 500 Fifth Avenue, New York, NY 10110

For information about special discounts for bulk purchases, please contact
W. W. Norton Special Sales at specialsales@wwnorton.com or 800-233-4830

Manufacturing by Versa Press
Book design by Allison Chi
Production manager: Devon Zahn

Countryman Press
www.countrymanpress.com

An imprint of W. W. Norton & Company, Inc.
500 Fifth Avenue, New York, NY 10110
www.wwnorton.com

978-1-6826-8778-9

10 9 8 7 6 5 4 3 2 1

"We will dine first, Hastings, and, until we drink our coffee, we will not discuss the case further. When engaged in eating, the brain should be the servant of the stomach."

—HERCULE POIROT, *Lord Edgware Dies*

# CONTENTS

# FOREWORD

A S early as 1901, when Agatha Miller was 11, she developed a love of cream: Devonshire cream, clotted cream, double cream; she drank combinations of these by the cup, and this addiction remained with her for life. Her "Author's Foreword" to *The Adventure of the Christmas Pudding* (1960) reminisces about the astonishingly lavish childhood Christmas dinners that she and her family enjoyed at Abney Hall, her sister Madge's home. The table groaned with oyster soup and turbot, roast turkey, boiled turkey, and sirloin of beef, plum pudding, mince pies, trifle, and chocolates. Despite, she assures her readers, appearing "delicate and skinny," she enjoyed more than one helping of everything and "neither felt, nor [was], sick." Her 50th book, *A Murder Is Announced* (1950), featured a cake first sampled by her at the home of her friends the Newmans, described as "rich, rich, of a melting richness," and the ingredients include "chocolate and much butter, and sugar and raisins," topped off with chocolate icing. She celebrated her 70th birthday with "rich hot lobster" and her 80th with a menu of avocado vinaigrette, lobster à la crème, blackberry ice cream, all washed down with a cup of neat cream!

Her guests also benefited from her love of food. In *The Mousetrap Man* (1972), Sir Peter Saunders, producer of *The Mousetrap*, describes the "delightful informality" of staying at Greenway House, with guests going down to breakfast "whenever they wished and helping themselves from heated trays on the sideboard." In *Memories of Men and Women* (1971), A. L. Rowse, fellow of All Souls College, Oxford, and a colleague of Max Mallowan, Agatha's second husband, recalls frequent visits to their home at Wallingford and records that "there was always good food and second helpings" of, for example, silverside and dumplings; conversations included debate about whether "milk, cream, butter, poultry, provisions" were easier in Oxfordshire or Devon. That said, Agatha welcomed Max Mallowan home from World War II with burnt kippers!

And food also had an additional aspect, one that is often overlooked. In the earliest book to consider the Christie phenomenon, *Agatha Christie: Mistress of Mystery* (1967), G. C. Ramsey includes a chapter on "Mystery Writers as Social Historian." He discusses the social and domestic detail that many detective novels include, almost as an aside. The number of servants, the use of real fires, the presence or absence of telephones and electric light—all these are features of Golden Age detective fiction, as is the presence of food.

Today, almost 50 years after her death, every aspect of Agatha Christie's life and career has been analyzed and pored over: her travels, her literary output, and the endless cycle of media adaptations it inspired. There have been quiz books, crossword books, graphic novels, poetry collections, as well as books exploring her jacket illustrations and cover designs, examining her use of poisons and her application of forensics. There are even, I hear, books analyzing her notebooks! But in all this range of associated work, little attention has been paid to an aspect of life important to everyone: food. And, as Karen will show in the following pages, this plays a significant part in all of Agatha Christie's work—and in Dame Agatha's own life.

I met Karen, appropriately, at a dining table; to be specific, Agatha Christie's dining-room table. It was during the annual International Agatha Christie Festival, held in Torquay every September, in honor of Dame Agatha's birthday, September 15. I was hosting the annual Greenway Dinner, held, not surprisingly, in Greenway House, Dame Agatha's holiday home since her purchase of the house in 1938. The dining table is boardroom-sized and seats at least 20 guests. Alongside is the sideboard where warming dishes—evident in some early Christie titles—kept food at an appetizing temperature, enabling weekend guests to arrive at whatever time suited them. And it is where Dame Agatha and her family celebrated Christmas and birthdays, family occasions and official meals, and everyday meals when guests stayed at the Georgian mansion and enjoyed country-house hospitality. It is also where the Folliatt and Stubbs families—and Hercule Poirot—dined during *Dead Man's Folly*.

Over dinner, Karen told me of her love of Agatha Christie and that she was working on an unofficial book that looked at Dame Agatha's use—and sometimes misuse!—of food. And it made me realize that this was a little-discussed part of the Christie output.

In her book, Karen acts as social historian. When you finish reading *Recipes for Murder*, you will know, inter alia, when hot food was first served on a plane, when the coffee percolator was invented, the genesis of Lobster Newburg, Pêche Melba, and Oysters Rockefeller, the situation re domestic servants during World War II, and the origins of the modern restaurant. And, as Karen shows, techniques of cooking the same food can vary over time: "recipes obey their moments in time." Along the way, you will learn the history of hot chocolate, the meaning of "grog," the arrival of the espresso machine, the origin of the cocktail, and the connection between Miss Marple and passion fruit and Agatha Christie and Elvis Presley!

As Karen entertainingly leads us through the "murder menus" of Agatha Christie, remember that dark deeds can take place in any "foodie" situation: the dinner table (*Three Act Tragedy*), a cocktail reception (*The Mirror Crack'd from Side to Side*), a casual lunch (*Sad Cypress*), a birthday party (*Sparkling Cyanide*), a Halloween celebration (*Hallowe'en Party*), or afternoon tea (*A Pocket Full of Rye*).

Whether you are a devotee of Agatha Christie and her ingenious murder mysteries or a food lover with a secret passion to become a gourmet chef, Karen's collection of *Recipes for Murder* will feed both enthusiasms.

—*Dr. John Curran*

# INTRODUCTION

"If you are going into exile, a good cook may be of
more comfort than a pretty face."

—HERCULE POIROT,
"The Adventure of Clapham Cook"

T HE third and youngest child of Frederick Miller, an American, and his wife, Clarissa (née Boehmer), a Briton, Agatha Miller was born on September 15, 1890, in Torquay, England. By her own account—in her autobiography, published posthumously—she "had a very happy childhood." Her siblings, Madge and Monty, preceded her by 11 and 10 years, respectively, so she spent much of her childhood alone. Her mother taught her to read, write, and do basic arithmetic at home, and little Agatha found companionship with her pets, imaginary friends, and books.

Learning to read by age 4, Agatha Miller absorbed everything she could, starting with Edith Nesbit, Lewis Carroll, and, later, Charles Dickens, William Wordsworth, and William Shakespeare. Soaking it all in, she wrote her first poem at age 10. By 18, she had written her first short story and begun work on *Snow upon the Desert*, her first novel. She never sold it, but she never stopped writing.

At age 24, she met and married Archibald Christie, a British military officer. During the Great War, he fought overseas, and she worked in the Torquay Red Cross Hospital, first as a nurse and later as a dispenser in the pharmacy. Here she formed a lifelong fascination with poisons, which guided her through many murders over the next 60 years. A fan of detective novels—which had begun in 1841 with "The Murders in the Rue Morgue" by Edgar Allan Poe, featuring French detective Auguste Dupin—and of Arthur Conan Doyle's subsequent Sherlock Holmes stories, Christie wrote *The Mysterious Affair at Styles*, her first detective novel, in 1916 at age 26. After Christie committed to writing five more books, British publisher John Lane published it in New York City in October

1920 and, under its Bodley Head imprint, in London in January 1921. A wife, mother, and now published author, Christie settled into life with her husband first in London and then in Sunningdale, Berkshire, a golfing suburb.

Like Hercule Poirot, who appears in her first detective novel, Christie loved good food, but this collection of recipes doesn't examine what she ate and drank herself. Rather, it examines the different ways she incorporates various meals, dishes, drinks, and ingredients into her novels. Occasionally she wields food as a weapon, but more often meals serve as plot devices. In her stories, food develops characters or invokes settings, whether familiar or foreign. Through 33 novels and more than 50 short stories, Poirot, with his sensitive but particular stomach, pursues gastronomic pleasure, regardless of the body count. You can do the same—evoking your favourite characters, scenes, or settings—by creating these dishes in your own kitchen.

The food mentioned in the Christie canon always has fascinated me, a lifelong devotee of detective fiction and a cooking enthusiast. I deduced—correctly, it seems—that others around the world must be as curious as I about marrows and marmalade, seedcake and lemon squash . . . and could the recipe for Mrs. MacDonald's Salmon Cream in Aunt Ada's desk really be made? This book looks at how Christie uses food in her novels, whether to advance plots or define characters, and examines the ingredients, the marrows and marmalades, that feature in them. Into a spreadsheet went all mentions of eating and drinking in each novel. As I researched, I noted how geography, servants, wars, and technology all made their mark on the changing world and the world of food throughout Christie's lifetime. Settings change from country manors with full contingents of servants, by way of a world war, to middle-class professionals' homes featuring the latest labour-saving devices.

After eliminating impossibly expert-level fare, I created a recipe for each novel that would prove easy enough for most home cooks and best represent the milieu of the novel. I scoured a variety of vintage cookbooks and other sources, including pestering family, friends, and neighbours for ideas and recipes, all of which I recreated and tested in my own kitchen. The recipes range from the proper way to make a cup of English tea or boil potatoes to preparing Dover sole and even, an Elvis Presley favourite, a grilled bacon and banana sandwich.

All the recipes obey their moments in time, following the standards of their respective eras. For Entrecôte à la Merlinville-sur-Mer (*The Murder on the Links*, 1923), the steak fries in lots of butter on the stovetop, but for Grilled Steak at the Golden Palm (*A Caribbean Mystery*, 1964), the recipe calls for marinade and an outdoor grill, each according to the place and style of its setting.

I decided on dishes central to plots or characters, and most recipes are both traditionally British and local to their settings, such as Welsh Cakes for *Why Didn't They Ask Evans?* or Fresh Windsor Soup, a common wartime stew featured in the postwar novel *Taken at the Flood*. But sometimes I've selected something decidedly un-British. For *The Secret Adversary*, I chose Pêche Melba, Tuppence Cowley's favourite dessert, which Auguste Escoffier, chef at the Savoy in London, created in honour of Australian opera singer Nellie Melba. Greek Rice Pilaf, another non-English dish, represents the murder victim's home country in *Crooked House*. *Death Comes as the End* takes place in ancient Egypt, and for that novel I found an ancient recipe for Tiger Nut Sweets, still made today.

The Christie Estate hasn't authorized this book, and all recipes are my own. I hope they will deepen your understanding of how Christie uses food in her books and allow you to appreciate her work in a new way. Though her father was American, Christie herself was British and of course used British spellings. I'm Canadian, and Canadian English shares many spellings with British English, which I have retained. But I studiously have avoided spoilers. If you haven't read a particular book or seen a screen adaptation of it, you may discover the identity of a victim or two—but never the murderer.

*Bon appétit, mes amis.*

1920s

THE death and destruction of the Great War ended in 1918. The smoke cleared, giving way to a decade of hedonism, celebration, and abandon. In the Jazz Age, everything changed—financially, domestically, and culturally. An astute observer, Christie documented these changes in her novels. In 1925, Lord Caterham hosts a typical country weekend in *The Secret of Chimneys* with a full complement of servants, including chauffeurs, nannies, and gardeners, with buffets for breakfast and formal dinners nightly. By 1929, in *The Seven Dials Mystery*, a self-made millionaire is renting the estate for the season. *The Man in the Brown Suit* (1924) tells the adventure story of Anne Beddingfeld, a plucky orphan pretending to be a journalist and hitching a ride to South Africa on the trail of diamonds and a master criminal. By 1928, in *The Mystery of the Blue Train*, the protagonist of that story works as a companion to an elderly lady, and it takes an inheritance for her to take a train to the South of France for a holiday.

As electricity and the labour-saving devices it powered slowly became commonplace in middle-class homes, the 1920s saw a decline of the servant classes. British homes now featured gas cookers, American-style refrigeration, bread toasters, and other devices that changed everyday kitchens forever. The best homes still had the best cooks but fewer kitchen maids, so fine dining evolved toward simpler, easier-to-prepare dishes. "A discreet revolution in food took place in the Twenties and Thirties," writes Arabella Boxer in her *Book of English Food*. "The criterion of good food was subtlety of flavour and contrast, combined with that perfection of simplicity, which is the hardest thing to achieve." Initially only "the moneyed upper classes and the intelligentsia" enjoyed these dishes, but soon these new ideas about food filtered down through society as the cooks that created them left their posts at great aristocratic homes to work in hotels and restaurants, where the middle and working classes could taste and enjoy them, too.

For Christie, the decade began auspiciously with her first published novel. Her happiness didn't last, however. The Roaring Twenties crashed onward, her mother died in 1926, and shortly afterward Christie's husband asked for a divorce to marry his mistress. In December of that year, Christie famously disappeared for 11 days. She reappeared at the Swan Hydropathic Hotel in Harrogate, Yorkshire, where she had checked in as Teresa Neele (her husband's mistress's surname) from Cape Town, South Africa. For the rest of her life, she never gave any explanation for her vanishing, and the motives for her destination and alias remain a mystery.

# A PERFECT
# CUP OF COFFEE

*"Mon ami* . . . somebody stepped on that cup, grinding it to powder, and the reason they did so was either because it contained strychnine or— which is far more serious—because it did not contain strychnine!"

—HERCULE POIROT, *The Mysterious Affair at Styles,* 1920

## ❧ SERVES 2 ❧

In the middle of the Great War, on a dare from her sister, Christie wrote *The Mysterious Affair at Styles*, her first published novel. She had grown up in a large house on the edge of a small town and worked in a hospital dispensary during the war. True to the adage "Write what you know," this story is about country life, the war, and poisons. Most importantly, it introduces Hercule Poirot, her most famous character. A celebrated, eccentric detective from the Belgian police force and a consummate gourmand, Poirot likes his coffee strong, prefers a tisane to English tea, and regards English cooking as bland, with few exceptions. In this mystery, the smashed coffee cup offers one of the first clues to the identity of the murderer. Joseph Laurens, a Parisian tinsmith, invented the first percolator a century earlier in 1819. At Styles, a country manor house, the after-dinner coffee would have come from such a percolator, but at the village guest house where Poirot and his fellow refugees live, the cook likely would have brewed the coffee using the new European drip method.

*continues*

## 4 heaping tablespoons coffee beans of choice for 4 tablespoons of grounds

1. Set a kettle filled with 2 cups (500 millilitres) of filtered water over high heat to boil.

2. While waiting for the water to boil, grind the beans in a coffee grinder to a medium grind, about 30 seconds, depending on the grinder.

3. Place a coffee filter over a small coffee pot and add the grounds to the center of the filter. Gently tap them to create an even surface.

4. When the water boils, remove the kettle from the heat and let it sit for 30 seconds.

5. Pour 1 ounce (30 millilitres) of hot water on the grounds and wait 30 more seconds.

6. Pour half of the remaining water in and let it sit for 30 more seconds.

7. Slowly pour the remaining water into the filter.

8. Serve 2 perfect cups of coffee as Poirot and his fellow refugees would enjoy.

# PÊCHE MELBA

"I have come into money, and the shock has been too much for me!
For that particular form of mental trouble an eminent physician
recommends unlimited Hors d'oeuvre, Lobster à l'américane,
Chicken Newberg, and Pêche Melba!"

—PRUDENCE "TUPPENCE" COWLEY,
*The Secret Adversary*, 1922

## ❧ SERVES 6 ❧

Christie's second novel introduces the detective team of Tommy and Tuppence. Reuniting after the Great War has ended, young Tommy Beresford and Tuppence Cowley dream of expensive treats and luxuries of the past, but they find themselves out of work and out of cash. They used to enjoy fabulous feasts, but now they live on tea and toast. To make money, they form the Young Adventurers Ltd., offering their services to do anything, anywhere, with "no unreasonable offer refused." Cowley's first adventure nets her a large number of £5 notes, and she tells Beresford to head to the Savoy or Ritz—any luxury hotel will do—for a fine meal. In 1894, Australian opera singer Nellie Melba performed in Covent Garden to rapturous acclaim. Duly impressed, Auguste Escoffier, chef of the Savoy Hotel, created Pêche Melba in her honour the next day. Tuppence's attitude toward fine dining will change, reflecting her values at various points in her life, we shall see, because Tommy and Tuppence age in real time through their series.

*continues*

1¾ cups (350 grams) granulated
   white sugar

2 teaspoons vanilla extract

3 whole cloves

1 cinnamon stick

3 large or 6 small peaches

2 cups (250 grams) raspberries,
   fresh or frozen

1 splash Chambord or other
   raspberry liqueur

6 large scoops vanilla ice cream

---

1. In a medium saucepan over medium-low heat, combine 2 cups (500 millilitres) water, 1½ cups (300 grams) sugar, the vanilla extract, cloves, and cinnamon stick and bring to a simmer.

2. While waiting for the mixture to simmer, peel the peaches, halve them, and discard the stones.

3. When the mixture simmers, use a large spoon to place the peach halves carefully in the saucepan. Continue simmering, uncovered, until tender, about 5 minutes.

4. Remove the pan from the heat and let it cool to room temperature, about 45 minutes.

5. Cover and refrigerate for at least 1 hour or up to 24 hours.

6. At least 1 hour before serving, remove the peaches from the refrigerator. Remove the cloves and cinnamon stick and discard or save for another use.

7. In a small saucepan over medium-low heat, add ¼ cup (60 millilitres) water and the raspberries and bring to a simmer.

8. Mash the berries, stir in ¼ cup (50 grams) sugar, and continue simmering for 5 minutes.

9. Remove the raspberry sauce from the heat and, using a spatula or wooden spoon, work the sauce through a fine mesh strainer into a small bowl.

10. Add the raspberry liqueur and let the sauce cool to room temperature, about 45 minutes.

11. Divide the vanilla ice cream among 6 bowls and place 1 or 2 peach halves, depending on size, on top.

12. Drizzle with the raspberry sauce and serve.

# ENTRECÔTE À LA MERLINVILLE-SUR-MER

"The first restaurant we came to assuaged the pangs of hunger with an excellent omelette, and an equally excellent entrecôte to follow."

—ARTHUR HASTINGS, *The Murder on the Links*, 1923

### ⁂ SERVES 2 ⁂

Christie loved setting her novels abroad, and this one tips her hat to France, known for its rich and flavourful food, which of course Poirot appreciates. The story opens with Poirot receiving an extraordinary summons from French businessman Paul Renauld. But by the time Poirot and Hastings arrive at the Villa Geneviève in Merlinville-sur-Mer, they find Renauld stabbed to death with an ornate letter opener and lying in a fresh grave on the edge of a nearby golf course. After solving the mystery and saving an innocent man from the gallows, Poirot and Hastings head back to town, where they enjoy an excellent meal. An entrecôte roast comes from the back of the rib roast. (Rib eye steaks also come from this cut.) These thin and boneless steaks also go by the names Scotch fillet or club steak. *Entrecôte* literally means "between the ribs," traditionally the ninth and eleventh ribs, making it a rare and particular treat.

2 entrecôte steaks

Salt and pepper

8 tablespoons (120 grams) unsalted
butter, cut in small pieces

2 shallots, finely chopped

½ cup (120 millilitres) red
Bordeaux wine

¾ cup (180 millilitres) reduced or
thickened beef stock

2 tablespoons chopped fresh parsley

1. Bring the steaks to room temperature and season them with salt and pepper to taste.

2. Heat a stainless steel or cast-iron skillet over medium-high heat until smoking hot.

3. Add 4 tablespoons (60 grams) of butter.

4. For rare steaks, sear them 2 minutes per side. For medium, 1 more minute per side.

5. Remove the steaks from the skillet, set them aside, and cover them with foil.

6. Reduce the heat to medium and, in the same pan, cook the shallots until they turn golden, about 7 or 8 minutes.

7. Pour in the wine to deglaze the skillet. Add the beef stock and stir well.

8. Simmer the sauce over medium-low heat until it reduces by half.

9. Stir in the remaining butter, 1 piece at a time. Let each piece melt fully before adding the next.

10. Carve the meat across the grain and arrange on serving plate.

11. Stir the parsley into the cooking sauce and pour a little over the meat. Pour the rest in a serving boat to accompany the steaks.

12. Pair with 2 glasses of the red Bordeaux.

# DRUG STORE COFFEE ICE CREAM SODA

"A man, I suppose, would have had a stiff peg; but girls derive
a lot of comfort from ice cream sodas."

—ANNE BEDDINGFELD, *The Man in the Brown Suit*, 1924

### ❧ SERVES 4 ❧

In 1922, Christie and her husband undertook a 10-month trade mission around the world to promote the British Empire Exhibition. Detailed letters collected in *The Grand Tour* reveal her spirit as fearless, bright, fun, and as ready for adventure as Anne Beddingfeld, the plucky heroine in *The Man in the Brown Suit*, who jumps at the chance to sail to South Africa. The novel also pokes fun at hard-boiled detectives such as Race Williams, the first hard-boiled private eye, written by Carroll John Daly. In December 1922, *Black Mask* magazine published Daly's "The False Burton Combs," the story that introduced Williams. After Miss Beddingfeld's ocean voyage to South Africa, she escapes her pursuers in Cape Town. Instead of recovering with a swig from an ever-present flask of whiskey, as Williams would have done, she finds the nearest drug store soda counter and orders two coffee ice cream sodas. Here's what the drug store may have served her.

3 cups (720 millilitres) A Perfect Cup of Coffee (page 3)

1–2 tablespoons granulated white sugar

1 teaspoon vanilla extract

1 cup (240 millilitres) single cream

½ cup (120 millilitres) heavy (double) cream

4 scoops vanilla ice cream

1 cup (240 millilitres) seltzer or sparkling water

Cocoa powder or grated chocolate for garnish

---

1. Make 3 cups of A Perfect Cup of Coffee.

2. Add the sugar, let the coffee cool to room temperature, then refrigerate for at least 1 hour.

3. In a large pitcher, mix the coffee with the vanilla extract and the single cream.

4. Divide the coffee mixture among 4 tall glasses, filling each about halfway.

5. In a medium bowl, add the heavy (double) cream and whip with a hand mixer or immersion blender until soft peaks form. Set aside.

6. Add 1 scoop of ice cream to each glass, followed by ¼ cup (60 millilitres) seltzer or sparkling water.

7. Divide the whipped cream among the glasses and garnish with cocoa powder or grated chocolate if desired.

8. Serve with a metal straw and apply yourself to the end of the straw with gusto!

# POACHED EGGS
# AT CHIMNEYS

"Eggs and bacon, kidneys, devilled bird, haddock, cold ham,
cold pheasant. I don't like any of these things, Tredwell.
Ask the cook to poach me an egg, will you?"

—CLEMENT BRENT, 9TH MARQUESS OF CATERHAM,
*The Secret of Chimneys*, 1925

### ❧ SERVES 1 ❧

When Lord Caterham of Chimneys, a country manor house, reluctantly agrees to host a shooting party for a visiting prince and his entourage, Tredwell, the butler, stands ready to meet the demands of the "week-end" in this madcap thriller with a secret society, stolen love letters, and a risqué memoir. The story features many meals: breakfast buffets, a shooting-party lunch, tea in the nursery with the French governess, and formal dinners. Yet Christie offers just one small glimpse of the food served. The breakfast buffet vaunts the host's status, meets the expected preferences of the time, and usually resembles dinner from the night before. The eggs would be scrambled and the bacon local. Cooks usually fried kidneys and served them in a spicy brown sauce. The deviled bird would have been leftover cold duck, turkey, or other gamebird served with a deviled cream sauce, made with heavy (double) cream, anchovies, dry mustard, and Worcestershire sauce. Haddock was a common fish to serve, the ham probably came from a local farm, and the gamekeeper would have shot and provided the pheasant. But it's all a bit much for the marquess. For the poached egg that he requests, the cook's secret is freshness—because older eggs break apart in the water—and vinegar.

**1 teaspoon vinegar**

**2 large eggs**

**Salt and pepper**

1. In a medium saucepan over medium heat, add 2 inches (5 centimetres) of water and the vinegar.

2. Into a small bowl or cup, crack 1 egg.

3. When tiny bubbles form on the bottom of the saucepan, gently pour the egg into the water, giving the egg a quick twist with a spoon. Repeat with the second egg.

4. Reduce the heat slightly and cook for 2–3 minutes, depending on the size of the eggs.

5. With a slotted spoon, gently lift each egg from the water and drain well.

6. Season with salt and pepper to taste and serve.

# STUFFED VEGETABLE MARROWS

"For some months now I cultivate the marrows. This morning
suddenly I enrage myself with these marrows. I send them to
promenade themselves—alas! Not only mentally but physically.
I seize the biggest. I hurl him over the wall."

—HERCULE POIROT, *The Murder of Roger Ackroyd*, 1926

### ⚜ SERVES 4-6 ⚜

In one of Christie's most controversial mysteries, Poirot has moved to King's
Abbot, a typical English village, in which reside a retired military man, a
businessman or two, a lawyer, quite a few single women, and of course a local
doctor. Living next door to Poirot are Dr. James Sheppard and his sister,
Caroline Sheppard. Christie acknowledges in her autobiography that Miss
Sheppard served as a precursor to Miss Marple. The novel opens with Poirot
retired from solving crime but obsessed with growing perfect marrows. In
a fit of frustration, the usually elegant and composed detective flings them
over the garden wall, accidentally assaulting Dr. Sheppard. Contrite for his
tantrum, Poirot begs forgiveness but never reveals his plans for the vegetable,
later presenting one to Miss Sheppard as a gift. Marrow, also called marrow
squash, is a popular vegetable in Britain. It's green, elongated, and resembles
its zucchini (courgette) sibling, with the same mild flavour. Because marrows
can prove hard to find if not grown—and with patience—this recipe makes use
of the marrow's more common sibling.

Salt

4–6 zucchini (courgettes)

4 cloves garlic

1 tablespoon finely chopped fresh sage

1 tablespoon finely chopped fresh thyme

½ tablespoon finely chopped fresh rosemary

1 pinch ground black pepper

1 tablespoon olive oil, plus more for greasing and brushing

1 large yellow onion, coarsely chopped

1 pound (450 grams) lean ground (mince) beef

1½ cups (360 millilitres) or one 19-ounce can (400 grams) diced tomatoes

1 tablespoon tomato paste

2 tablespoons finely chopped fresh parsley

1 large egg

2 ounces (60 grams) Parmesan cheese, grated

2 ounces (60 grams) pecorino cheese, grated

---

1. Preheat the oven to 350°F (180°C).

2. Bring a large pot of lightly salted water to a boil.

3. While waiting for the water to boil, cut the zucchini in half lengthwise and remove any seeds or pulp. Carve a U-shaped valley along the length. Reserve the seeds and pulp.

4. When the water boils, add the zucchini halves to the pot. Turn the heat off and let them sit in the water for 5–10 minutes to soften.

5. Remove the zucchini from the water and drain. Set aside.

6. Crush or grate the garlic and add it to a small bowl, followed by the sage, thyme, rosemary, black pepper, and a pinch of salt.

*continues*

7.  In a large frying pan over low heat, add the olive oil and onions and cook until they become soft and translucent, about 10 minutes.

8.  Add the garlic herb mixture to the onions and stir well.

9.  Increase the heat to medium, add the beef, and cook for 10 more minutes, stirring regularly until the beef browns.

10. While cooking the beef, chop the reserved zucchini seeds and pulp.

11. After the beef has cooked for 10 minutes, add the chopped zucchini seeds and pulp, diced tomatoes, and tomato paste. Cook for another 10 minutes, stirring occasionally.

12. Add half the parsley, stir, and remove the pan from the heat.

13. Let the stuffing mixture cool for 10 minutes. While it's cooling, beat the egg.

14. When the mixture has cooled, add the egg and half of each cheese and stir until well combined.

15. Grease a broad casserole or roasting dish with a little olive oil and add the cored zucchini halves, cut sides up.

16. Brush the tops of the cored zucchini with olive oil, fill with the stuffing mixture, and sprinkle with most of the remaining cheese.

17. Bake for 30–40 minutes, until the top of the cheese turns golden brown.

18. Let the stuffed zucchini rest for 5 minutes.

19. Sprinkle the remaining cheese and parsley over the zucchini, serve, and pair with a bottle of Chardonnay.

# SUNDAY ROAST
# LEG OF LAMB

"Everybody swore that no one had been to the Granite Bungalow
that morning, but, nevertheless, I found in the larder a leg of mutton,
still frozen. It was Monday, so the meat must have been delivered that
morning; for if on Saturday, in this hot weather, it would not have
remained frozen over Sunday."

—HERCULE POIROT, *The Big Four*, 1927

### ⅍ SERVES 4 ⅍

*The Big Four* began as a collection of short stories before becoming a novel featuring four master criminals: an American millionaire, a French scientist, a Chinese genius, and an unknown master of disguise. Together and separately, they pit their wits against Hercule Poirot in a bid for world domination. The detective's investigation begins slowly. The only witness he can find turns up dead, though he has plenty of footprints and trails of blood to follow. Then the famous sleuth discovers a culinary clue: a frozen leg of mutton. The delivery must have happened not only that morning but also by someone on whom a trace of blood would attract no attention. When properly defrosted and not serving as a murder clue, a leg of lamb makes an excellent Sunday roast, a beloved British tradition for the whole family. The meal features roasted meat, potatoes, and vegetables served with condiments such as mint sauce, currant jelly, and apple sauce and other accompaniments, including onion sauce, gravy, and Yorkshire puddings.

*continues*

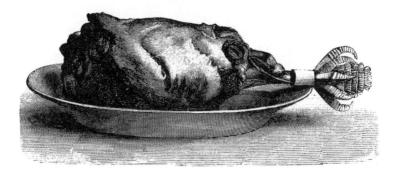

1 tablespoon chopped fresh
  rosemary, plus several sprigs

Zest of 1 medium lemon

2 tablespoons olive oil

4½-pound (2-kilogram) leg of
  lamb, bone in

Salt and pepper

¼ cup (16 grams) finely chopped
  fresh mint

1 teaspoon granulated white sugar

3 tablespoons white wine vinegar

---

1.   Preheat the oven to 400°F (200°C).

2.   In a small bowl, mix the chopped rosemary, lemon zest, and olive oil.

3.   Season the lamb with salt and pepper to taste, then coat it with the herb mixture.

4.   In a large roasting pan, add the lamb and rosemary sprigs.

5.   Roast for 1 hour 15 minutes.

6.   While the lamb is roasting, make the mint sauce. In a small bowl, mix the mint, sugar, 2 pinches of salt, vinegar, and 1 tablespoon hot water. Set aside.

7.   When the lamb finishes roasting, let it rest, covered, for at least 15 minutes before carving. Discard the roasted rosemary sprigs and garnish with fresh sprigs.

8.   Serve with the mint sauce and pair with a bottle of Syrah.

# LITTLE CASTLE PUDDINGS

"It is no good having a tart because she is heavy handed with pastry; but her little castle puddings are not bad."

—AMELIA VINER, *The Mystery of the Blue Train*, 1928

### ❧ SERVES 6 ❧

After a windfall inheritance, Katherine Grey, a slightly older but still spirited woman from St. Mary Mead, travels on the famed *Blue Train* to spend the winter in France. At this time, the train offers no dining service, so passengers order lunch or dinner baskets at a station. In the 1920s, the restaurant in the Gare de Lyon was one of the best in Paris, and a first-class dinner basket would have been a delight. Back in St. Mary Mead, Katherine asks her elderly friend Miss Viner whether she can invite one of her handsome suitors from the Riviera to dine with them. Is the K on the cigarette case for Derek Kettering or Major Knighton? For either gentleman, proper dinner would require too much effort and expenditure, so Miss Grey wisely settles on lunch while Miss Viner details the limits of her cook's abilities and what kind of meal to serve to such a gentleman. Miss Viner, a spinster, has preserved much of her father's wine collection for just such an occasion and suggests "a bottle of sparkling Moselle, perhaps," today known as a Crémant de Luxembourg. For dessert or pudding (as the British call the category), Ellen, the cook, might not make these lovely cakes very well, but this recipe will ensure that you can.

*continues*

½ cup (115 grams) salted butter, room temperature, plus more for greasing

½ cup (100 grams) granulated white sugar

2 large eggs

½ teaspoon vanilla extract

½ cup (60 grams) bleached all-purpose (white) flour

½ teaspoon baking powder

Fifth Column Blackberry Jam (page 73) or Orange Marmalade from Gossington Hall (page 75)

Crème fraîche

---

1. Preheat the oven to 350°F (200°C).

2. Lightly grease ramekins or muffin tins.

3. With a stand mixer, cream the butter and sugar until light and fluffy.

4. While creaming the butter and sugar, beat the eggs in a small bowl.

5. Add the beaten eggs and vanilla to the creamed butter and mix for another few minutes, until well combined.

6. In another small bowl, sift together the flour and baking powder.

7. Fold the flour mixture into the batter and stir gently until it combines fully.

8. Spoon the batter into the ramekins or muffin tins, about ¾ full.

9. Bake for 18–22 minutes, until set. Toothpick-test for doneness. (A toothpick inserted in the center should come out clean.)

10. While the cakes are baking, warm the jam or marmalade.

11. Serve with crème fraîche and the warm jam or marmalade.

# FISH AND CHIPS AT THE SEVEN DIALS CLUB

> "Used to be a slummy sort of district round about Tottenham Court Road way. It's all pulled down and cleaned up now. But the Seven Dials Club keeps to the old atmosphere. Fried fish and chips."
>
> —BILL EVERSLEIGH, *The Seven Dials Mystery*, 1929

### ❧ SERVES 4 ❧

Lord Caterham of Chimneys has leased his country estate for the season to Sir Oswald Coote, a self-made millionaire, and his wife. Unfortunately, the season included several "young things," a good joke gone wrong, and a dead body. Returning home, the marquess expects peace and quiet, but his daughter, Lady Eileen "Bundle" Brent, finds a mysterious, unfinished letter written by the guest who died. It warns its intended recipient to forget about "that Seven Dials business." Bundle Brent investigates, becoming embroiled in a madcap mystery. Before she can leave Chimneys for the Seven Dials neighbourhood of London, another Chimneys guest runs in front of her car and collapses, whispering "Seven Dials" as his dying words. Bundle's friend Bill Eversleigh describes 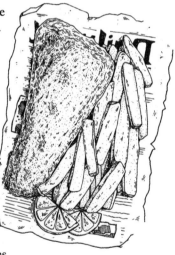 the recent gentrification of this part of London, and she immediately insists on going, not just to solve the mystery but to dine on the club's signature down-market dish. Fish and chips have become an iconic British staple instantly

*continues*

recognizable around the world, but the halves of this dish came to Britain separately. Batter-fried fish came first, brought by the descendants of Jews expelled from Spain and Portugal. Fried potatoes, which the British call "chips," seem to have arisen in the early days of the Victorian era. Oldham, near Manchester, lays claim to the kingdom's first chip shop, and by the middle of the era, a community of Belgian immigrants was selling fried potatoes in Dundee, Scotland. Exactly how and when fish and chips joined forces remains a mystery.

3 pounds (1.3 kilograms) potatoes

Oil for frying

¾ cup (90 grams) bleached all-purpose (white) flour, plus more for dusting

1 teaspoon baking soda

Salt and pepper

1 bottle Newcastle Brown Ale or other English ale

1 tablespoon malt vinegar

4 fillets cod, haddock, or halibut, skinless and pin-boned

1. Peel the potatoes and cut them into fries or, as the British say, chips.

2. Pour enough oil into an electric deep fryer to fill it about 3 inches (8 centimetres) deep and heat to 300°F (150°C).

3. Use a wire basket or slotted spoon to lower the potatoes into the oil. Fry for 4–5 minutes, until the potatoes soften but don't brown.

4. Remove the potatoes, drain, and set aside.

5. Increase the heat to 375°F (190°C).

6. In a large bowl, mix the flour, baking soda, and salt and pepper to taste.

7. To the flour mixture, gradually add the ale and malt vinegar and whisk until smooth.

8. Dust the fish fillets with a little flour, then dip each into the batter, allowing any excess to drip off.

9. Carefully lower 1 fillet at a time into the fryer and cook until golden and crisp, about 4 minutes each. Drain.

10. Put the fries back in the fryer until they turn golden and crisp, about 3–4 minutes. Remove and drain again.

11. Divide the fish and chips among 4 plates, serve with salt and malt vinegar, and pair with more English ale.

NOTE: *If you don't have an electric fryer, use a deep, heavy-bottomed pot and a deep-fry thermometer to make the chips Seven Dials delicious.*

1930s

HOT on the heels of the great crash of 1929, this decade began amid financial devastation, setting the world on the bloody path to war again. Technological advancements in a variety of fields gave rise to more labour-saving devices, making housework easier, simpler, and safer. These innovations improved life but also changed it drastically. Electric ovens don't require kitchen maids to tend them constantly, so the role of housewife began transitioning from overseeing the running of a household to running it directly. The majority of household tasks now fell to the woman of the house, who had to make do with a much-reduced workforce.

In *The Murder at the Vicarage*, the vicarage has a bad cook, but they go to great lengths to accommodate her, lest she leave. *The Sittaford Mystery* features newly built cottages for two. A large family home sits empty in *Peril at End House*. Wealthier characters make do with one or two servants and entertain at fashionable hotels, as Lady Edgware does in *Lord Edgware Dies*. In *Appointment with Death*, the Borden family celebrates at the Savoy, but in smaller households, the characters cook for themselves.

By decade's end, village life has changed dramatically. In *Murder is Easy*, the manor house still has a few live-in servants, but most work part time and live in the village. Professional households, including the doctor's, function with just one full-time servant and maybe one or two daily servants. Most middle-class households have only daily or part-time help from cooks, cleaners, and chauffeurs, who have their own homes and families in the growing community.

Christie lived a little bit differently. She loved real estate and, in this decade, bought several homes. At one point, she owned eight houses in and around London. She lived in some but let family and friends stay in others. She also spent at least half the year on archaeological digs with Max Mallowan, whom she married in 1930. Her daughter, Rosalind Christie, lived in boarding schools for most of the year, and the family spent summer holidays at Ashfield, Christie's childhood home, which she now owned. Christie finally sold Ashfield in 1938 and purchased Greenway House in Devon. She left no clues, but perhaps her personal servants traveled with her, with daily household help hired for whichever home she was occupying at the time.

# OLD-FASHIONED RICE PUDDING

"Mary entered at that moment with a partially cooked rice pudding.
I made a mild protest, but Griselda said that the Japanese always ate
half-cooked rice and had marvellous brains in consequence."

—LEONARD CLEMENT, *The Murder at the Vicarage*, 1930

### ⁑ SERVES 6 ⁑

Known for her sharp mind and uncanny understanding of people's actions, Miss Marple of St. Mary Mead remains one of fiction's most famous and unusual detectives. Christie loosely based the spinster on her grandmothers and the ladies in the villages where she lived and visited as a child. Miss Marple eventually featured in 12 novels, this being the first, and 20 short stories. In this mystery, the vicar's cook, Mary, while not terribly good at her job, is still a valuable member of the staff. She boils beef until hard, burns puddings to a crisp, and serves undercooked beans, making her a prime suspect in any poisoning. The Reverend Leonard Clement valiantly protests Mary's rice pudding, but

his wife, Griselda, delights in the sunny side of life. After their exchange, the vicar no doubt sighed and ate his pudding without further fuss. Properly cooked rice pudding tastes lovely, so, in lieu of Mary's questionable version, here's a version closer to what Miss Marple might have made for her nephew, Raymond West.

*continues*

3½ ounces (100 grams) dessert or pudding rice

1¾ ounces (50 grams) granulated white sugar

Salted butter for greasing

1 pinch ground nutmeg

3 cups (700 millilitres) whole milk

1. Preheat the oven to 300°C (150°C).

2. Thoroughly wash and drain the rice.

3. Grease a 6-inch (15-centimetre) round baking dish or an 8-by-4-inch (20-by-10-centimetre) loaf pan and pour in the milk.

4. Add the rice and sugar and stir thoroughly. Sprinkle the nutmeg on top.

5. Cook for 1 hour 40 minutes to 2 hours, until the pudding wobbles just slightly when shaken.

6. Serve warm or cool to room temperature, refrigerate, and serve cold.

———•❂❊❂•———

NOTE: *Optional toppings include jam, sliced fruit, brown sugar, or maple syrup. Before cooking, you also can add raisins, vanilla extract, ground cinnamon, or lemon zest.*

# BRITISH COFFEE CAKE

"I hear you had the most delicious coffee cake for tea yesterday afternoon. Will you be so very kind as to give me the recipe for it. I know you'll not mind my asking you this—an invalid has so little variety except in her diet."

—CAROLINE PERCEHOUSE, *The Sittaford Mystery,* 1931

### ❧ YIELDS TWO 9-INCH (22-CENTIMETRE) ROUND CAKES ❧

Set in winter on the edge of Dartmoor in southwest England, this thriller features Australians, an escaped convict, newspaper puzzles, and a séance that foretells a murder. When Captain Joseph Trevelyan turns up dead and James Pearson, the fiancé of Emily Trefusis, stands accused of the crime, she heads to the nearby village of Sittaford to do some sleuthing. At one point, she needs a pretense to snoop at the manor house, and her hostess lends a hand by using this coffee cake recipe to draw out a suspect. British and American coffee cakes differ significantly. The British version contains coffee, while the sweeter American variety doesn't, often flavoured with fruits or cinnamon and meant to be served *with* coffee. This recipe uses Camp Coffee, a Scottish coffee syrup often used in baking. Serve it with vanilla ice cream or, better yet, hazelnut ice cream for a little variety.

*continues*

2¼ cups (270 grams) all-purpose (white) flour

4½ teaspoons baking powder

¼ teaspoon salt

1⅛ cups (255 grams) unsalted butter, softened, plus more for greasing

⅜ cup (85 grams) vegetable shortening

1½ cups (300 grams) granulated white sugar

5 large eggs

5 cups (1.2 litres) whole milk, plus 2 tablespoons

5½ tablespoons Camp Coffee, plus 2–3 tablespoons

4 cups (520 grams) confectioners' (powdered or icing) sugar

---

1. Preheat the oven to 375°F (190°C).

2. In a large bowl, sift together the flour, baking powder, and salt.

3. In a stand mixer fitted with a medium bowl, cream ⅜ cup (85 grams) of the butter, the shortening, and the sugar.

4. Add the eggs and beat well.

5. Add the milk and mix well.

6. Add 5½ tablespoons Camp Coffee, mixing well.

7. Grease two 9-inch (22-centimetre) round pans, divide the batter between them, and bake for 20–25 minutes.

8. While the cakes are baking, make the icing. With a hand mixer in a medium bowl, combine the confectioners' sugar with the remaining Camp Coffee and the remaining ¾ cup (170 grams) of butter. If the icing seems too thick, add the remaining milk and mix well. If too runny, add a little more confectioners' sugar. Mix until you achieve the desired consistency.

9. When the cakes have finished baking, toothpick-test them for doneness and let them cool to room temperature.

10. After the cakes have cooled, ice them in layers with all the icing.

# REGATTA
# LOBSTER NEWBURG

"I'm giving a party on Monday. It's Regatta Week, you know."

—MAGDALA BUCKLEY, *Peril at End House*, 1932

## ✤ SERVES 4 ✤

While on holiday at the Majestic Hotel in St. Loo, Cornwall—based on the Imperial Hotel, Torquay—Poirot and Hastings meet Magdala "Nick" Buckley, a modern young woman who lives in End House, a slightly ramshackle manor on the point. Poirot believes that Buckley's life lies in danger, and when a murder occurs at her Regatta Week party, he and Hastings become embroiled in the investigation. During a regatta—a social series of boat races, from the Venetian word *regata*, or "contest"—gentry host fancy dinner parties, families picnic near the water, and everyone has a drink in the pub. Regatta Week in St. Loo takes its lead from Cowes Week, founded in 1826 by King George IV. To celebrate, Buckley has planned a dinner party to watch the fireworks. She has extravagant taste, a big mortgage, and only the locals to hire. For the party, she served traditional dishes using fresh, local food cooked by Ellen, her housekeeper. Lobster Newburg, an American dish, debuted in 1876 at Delmonico's Restaurant in Manhattan. Instantly popular, it quickly appeared on seaside menus on both sides of the Atlantic. Ellen's version, a favourite with all Buckley's guests, would use the plentiful Cornish lobster.

*continues*

¼ cup (60 grams) unsalted butter

2⅓ tablespoons dry Sherry

3⅓ tablespoons brandy

1½ cups (375 millilitres) heavy
 (double) cream

¼ teaspoon freshly grated nutmeg

**Cayenne pepper and salt**

**4 large egg yolks**

**2 pounds meat from cooked
 Cornish lobsters**

**Sliced bread for toast**

---

1. In a medium saucepan over low heat, melt the butter and add 2 table-spoons Sherry and 3 tablespoons brandy. Cook, stirring constantly, for 2 minutes.

2. Add the cream to the butter mixture and simmer until the volume reduces to about 1 cup (240 millilitres).

3. Reduce the heat to low. Stir in the nutmeg, the remaining teaspoon of Sherry, and the remaining teaspoon of brandy. Add cayenne pepper and salt to taste.

4. In a small bowl, beat the egg yolks well and add them to the mixture, whisking constantly for 3 minutes.

5. Remove the saucepan from the heat and stir in the lobster meat, mixing well.

6. Toast the bread and halve the slices diagonally.

7. On each plate, place 1 or 2 slices of toast, arrange the lobster mixture on the slices, and spoon the cooking sauce over top. Serve immediately.

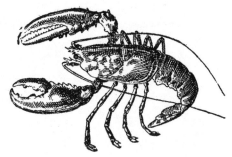

# SOHO BABA
# AU RHUM

"We went to a little restaurant in Soho where he was well known, and there we had a delicious omelette, a sole, a chicken, and a Baba au Rhum of which Poirot was inordinately fond."

—ARTHUR HASTINGS, *Lord Edgware Dies*, 1933

### ❧ YIELDS 6-8 CAKES ❧

The modern restaurant emerged after the French Revolution, when the newly unemployed chefs of the Ancien Régime started providing dining services for citizens of the First Republic. In the 1930s, the British aristocracy shifted to hosting social events at large hotels, which offered first-class food, obviating the need for the moneyed classes to maintain large town houses manned by an army of servants. After a theater performance, this mystery begins with a supper party at the Savoy hosted by Jane Wilkinson, a beautiful American actress married to Lord Edgware. Smaller groups, including Poirot and Hastings, patronized smaller, quality establishments, such as the Soho restaurant where Poirot, a regular, knows both owner and chef. The original Baba au Rhum recipe, invented in Paris in the 1830s, can prove particularly complicated, so here's an easier version.

*continues*

¾ cup (130 grams) golden raisins (sultanas)

11/16 cup (165 millilitres) dark rum

¼ cup (60 grams) butter, plus more for greasing

1 cup (120 grams) all-purpose (white) flour

2 teaspoons baking powder

1 tablespoon orange zest

1 teaspoon lemon zest

3 eggs

1⅔ cups (335 grams) granulated white sugar

¼ cup (60 millilitres) whole milk

½ teaspoon vanilla extract

⅔ cup (215 grams) apricot preserves

Whipped cream

---

1. Preheat the oven to 350°F (180°C).

2. In a small bowl, soak the raisins in 3 tablespoons dark rum.

3. Grease small ring molds or baba molds.

4. In a medium saucepan over low heat, melt the rest of the butter and set aside.

5. In another small bowl, sift together the flour and baking powder.

6. Stir the citrus zests and rum-soaked raisins into the flour mixture.

7. Separate the egg yolks from the whites.

8. With a hand mixer, beat the yolks with ⅔ cup (135 grams) sugar for 2 minutes.

9. Combine the flour mixture, melted butter, and milk, mixing in the yolk-sugar mixture until well combined.

10. With a hand mixer, beat the egg whites into stiff peaks.

11. Carefully and slowly fold the egg whites into the batter.

12. Divide the batter among the greased molds and bake for 15 minutes.

13. Let the cakes cool and turn them out onto plates.

14. Carefully prick the cakes several times with a skewer.

15. While the babas cool, make the rum soaking syrup. In a small saucepan over medium heat, boil ⅔ cup (160 millilitres) water and 1 cup (200 grams) sugar for 5–10 minutes, until the syrup thickens.

16. Remove the syrup from the heat and add the remaining ½ cup (120 millilitres) dark rum and vanilla extract.

17. In another small saucepan over low heat, gently warm the apricot preserves.

18. Spoon the hot rum syrup onto the babas, allowing them to soak it up. Repeat until they have absorbed all the syrup.

19. Carefully transfer each baba onto a dessert plate and brush them with the warm apricot preserves.

20. Top with whipped cream cream, garnish with a golden raisin, and serve warm.

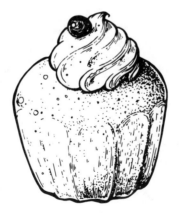

# OYSTERS ROCKEFELLER ON THE *ORIENT EXPRESS*

"Poirot sat down and soon found himself in the favoured position of being at the table which was served first and with the choicest morsels. The food, too, was unusually good."

—from *Murder on the* Orient Express, 1934

## ❧ SERVES 6 ❧

Created in 1883 by a Belgian train company, the *Orient Express* long-distance passenger service ran from Paris to Istanbul, renowned for its luxurious sleeper suites and high-quality cuisine. Six years later, at Antoine's restaurant in New Orleans, Jules Alciatore ran out of snails for escargot. In a pinch, he created Oysters Rockefeller, naming the dish for the founder of the Standard Oil Company, the richest American of the day. It was a pairing meant to be. In 1928, Christie booked passage on the *Orient Express* on her way to the Mandate for Mesopotamia (now Iraq). She became a regular traveler on the service, bringing her typewriter with her. The train offered Belgian chocolates, French cheeses and foie gras, Irish oysters, Russian caviar, and Scottish smoked salmon. Inspired by the 1932 abduction and murder of Charles Lindbergh Jr., son of the famous American aviator, this mystery first appeared serially as *Murder in the Calais Coach* and remains one of Christie's most well-known novels.

24 fresh oysters

2 cloves garlic

1 cup (30 grams) fresh spinach

2 teaspoons fresh lemon juice

½ cup (115 grams) unsalted butter, softened

2 tablespoons Pernod

¾ cup (110 grams) dried breadcrumbs

¼ cup (25 grams) grated Parmesan cheese

1 tablespoon extra-virgin olive oil, plus more for processing (if needed)

Coarse salt (optional)

3 lemons

---

1. Preheat the oven to 450°F (230°C).

2. With a shucking knife, open the oysters and cut the meat from the shells into a small bowl. Discard the flatter top shells and reserve the deeper bottom shells. Set aside.

3. In a food processor, purée the garlic, spinach, lemon juice, butter, and Pernod. Add a little olive oil if needed.

*continues*

4. In a medium bowl, combine the breadcrumbs, cheese, and olive oil. Set aside.

5. To level the oyster shells for ease of serving, spread coarse salt evenly in a baking sheet to a depth of ½ inch (1 centimetre). A large cupcake baking pan makes an eye-catching alternative.

6. Arrange the reserved oyster shells on the sheet or pan. Place 1 raw oyster in each shell.

7. Divide the purée among the oysters and top each with approximately 1 tablespoon of the breadcrumb mixture.

8. Bake until the mixture bubbles, about 8 minutes.

9. Quarter the lemons.

10. Plate the oysters for serving and garnish each plate with 2 lemon wedges.

# WELSH CAKES

"But Frankie and her brothers were not asked to the vicarage.
It seemed to be tacitly recognized that it would not be amusing
for them. . . . The two families had now nothing in common
save certain childish memories."

—from *Why Didn't They Ask Evans?*, 1934

### ❧ YIELDS 20 CAKES ❧

While playing golf with the local doctor, Bobby Jones, the
vicar's son, discovers a fatally injured man, who,
just before dying, whispers, "Why didn't they
ask Evans?" Not long afterward, Jones finds
himself in a railway carriage with Lady Fran-
ces "Frankie" Derwent, the daughter of Lord
Marchington of Marchbolt Castle in Wales.
Frankie, Jones, and their respective siblings grew
up in the village as childhood friends. When Frankie
and her brothers visit their parents, Bobby and his
brothers visit the castle and perhaps play tennis, but
the old friends now have little in common except for
shared memories of childhood. One of which no
doubt included eating Welsh cakes, a traditional
Christmas treat enjoyed by nobility and com-
moners alike.

*continues*

¼ cup (60 grams) salted butter, plus more for greasing (optional)

¼ cup (60 grams) vegetable shortening

2 ounces (60 grams) raisins

1½ cups (180 grams) bleached all-purpose (white) flour, plus more for dusting

1 teaspoon baking powder

⅓ cup (70 grams) granulated white sugar, plus more for sprinkling

1 large egg

1 tablespoon whole milk

Cinnamon for sprinkling

Fifth Column Blackberry Jam (page 73) or Orange Marmalade from Gossington Hall (page 75) (optional)

---

1. Cut the butter and shortening into small pieces and coarsely chop the raisins.

2. If you have a large pizza stone, grease it with butter and set it in the oven at 300°F (150°C). Alternatively, you can cook the Welsh cakes on the stovetop.

3. In a medium bowl, sift together the flour and baking powder.

4. Cut in the butter and shortening until the dough has the consistency of breadcrumbs.

5. With a wooden spoon, stir in the sugar and raisins.

6. Beat the egg and work it and the milk into the mixture. The dough should feel soft but still stiff enough to roll out. Add more milk or flour as necessary.

7. Lightly flour your work surface and roll out the dough to ⅛ inch (½ centimetre) thick.

8. With a cookie cutter or upside-down glass, cut out 3-inch (8-centimetre) circles. Reroll the trimmings and repeat until you use all the dough.

9. Carefully place the dough circles on the hot pizza stone and return it to the oven. If making the cakes on the stovetop, in a large nonstick

frying pan over low heat, fry the cakes for 5–6 minutes per side, until golden brown.

10. Sprinkle with sugar or cinnamon or both.

11. If desired, spread with Fifth Column Blackberry Jam or Orange Marmalade from Gossington Hall.

# CANAPÉS DIANE

> "'This is the menu for dinner. I don't know whether you would like it altered in any way.'
>
> Sir Charles took it and murmured:
>
> 'Let's see. Melon Cantaloupe, Borscht Soup, Fresh Mackerel, Grouse, Soufflé Surprise, Canapé Diane.... No, I think that will do excellently.'"
>
> —MISS MILRAY AND CHARLES CARTWRIGHT,
> *Three Act Tragedy*, 1934

### ❧ SERVES 8 ❧

Christie commits murder with food in all three acts of this mystery: a poisoned cocktail in the first act, a poisoned glass of Port in the second, and a poisoned box of chocolates in the final act. Sir Charles Cartwright, a retired actor, has invited 12 guests, including Poirot, for dinner at Crow's Nest, his seaside home in Cornwall. Miss Milray, his assistant, has planned an excellent meal to impress his friends and acquaintances. The menu includes canapés Diane, a French dish created in the 1850s. Traditional English dinner parties of the 1930s commonly featured this popular appetizer of chicken livers and bacon on toast. But contrary to tradition and popular superstition, 13 came for dinner that evening, a particularly unlucky turn for the local vicar, who drinks a poisoned cocktail and dies.

½ pound (225 grams) thick-sliced bacon

1 pound (450 grams) fresh chicken livers

French bread

1. Preheat the oven to broil.

2. Halve the bacon and the livers.

3. In a medium cast-iron skillet over medium-low heat, lightly cook the bacon, about 5 minutes. When done, the bacon should feel pliable. Remove from the skillet and drain on paper towels.

4. Wrap 1 piece of bacon around 1 piece of liver and secure with a toothpick. Repeat with remaining bacon and livers.

5. Place the bacon-wrapped livers on a large baking sheet and broil them for 6–8 minutes.

6. Turn them over and repeat until the bacon cooks well and becomes crispy on both sides.

7. While the bacon-wrapped livers are cooking, slice and toast the French bread.

8. Place the bacon-wrapped livers on the toast and serve.

# PROMETHEUS
# LOBSTER SALAD

"'Do each of you serve separate cars?'

'No, sir, we work it together. The soup, then the meat and vegetables and salad, then the sweet, and so on. We usually serve the rear car first, then go out with a fresh lot of dishes to the front car.'"

—HERCULE POIROT AND ALBERT DAVIS,
*Death in the Clouds*, 1935

### ❦ SERVES 2 ❦

Poirot is flying from Paris to Croydon, south of London. The flight's elaborate meal service, with its protracted routine, hides the murder of a French money-lender in plain sight. Flights from London to Paris first served meals in 1919, but on-board kitchens didn't come along until 1936, so airlines served these large and fashionable meals cold. Companies looking to attract wealthy passengers offered the best fare available. Stewards in white coats served such delicacies as vichyssoise, lobster salad, cold chicken and ham, cakes, and cheese with biscuits, all on fine china with linens and silver. They also provided Champagne, wine, mineral water, and coffee. This elaborate service showcased the luxury and elegance of air travel, but this time it also hides the murderer's movements. As Davis, the younger steward on the *Prometheus*, explains to Poirot, both stewards serve the rear cabin first. The last time Davis saw the moneylender alive was while serving cheese and biscuits, the final course.

¾ pound (340 grams) cooked lobster, cut in chunks

2 tablespoons mayonnaise

1 tablespoon fresh lemon juice

1 tablespoon finely chopped shallots or chives

1 tablespoon finely chopped fresh tarragon

Salt and pepper

2 large leaves butter lettuce

1 lemon

1. In a large bowl, add the lobster, mayonnaise, lemon juice, shallots or chives, and tarragon. Add salt and pepper to taste and mix well.

2. Place 1 lettuce leaf on each plate and top with lobster salad.

3. Garnish with a lemon wedge.

# MACARONI AU GRATIN AT THE GINGER CAT CAFÉ

"It was the kind of place that specialized in morning coffee, five different kinds of teas . . . and a few sparing lunch dishes for females such as scrambled eggs and shrimps and macaroni au gratin."

—ARTHUR HASTINGS, *The A.B.C. Murders*, 1936

### ⁑ SERVES 6 ⁑

Calling himself "A.B.C.," a killer taunts Poirot. Poirot and Hastings follow the trail from Alice Asher's tobacco shop in Andover to Bexhill-on-Sea, where the second murder victim, Betty Barnard, lived and worked as a waitress at the Ginger Cat Café. A tearoom of this era offered middle-class diners a nice place to lunch with friends while avoiding the beer and smoke of pubs and the fried offerings of lunchrooms catering to the working classes. The tradition of pasta and cheese for lunch dates to medieval times. A richer version, likely originating in France, used a béchamel cheese sauce and became a great favourite with the English. The Edwardians made it *au gratin* with a topping of buttered breadcrumbs. By the 1930s, it had become a staple in every tearoom in England.

¼ cup (60 grams) salted butter, plus more for greasing

½ pound (225 grams) uncooked elbow macaroni

¼ cup (30 grams) bleached all-purpose (white) flour

2 cups (500 millilitres) whole milk

½ pound (225 grams) Cheddar cheese, grated

1 tablespoon finely chopped shallot

½ teaspoon Worcestershire sauce

½ teaspoon salt

¼ teaspoon ground black pepper

¼ teaspoon powdered English mustard

2 tablespoons fine seasoned breadcrumbs

1. Preheat the oven to 375°F (190°C).

2. Grease a 2-quart (2-litre) casserole dish.

3. In a large pot, cook the macaroni according to the package directions. Drain and return to the pot.

4. In a large saucepan over medium heat, melt the butter. Stir in the flour, mixing well.

5. Gradually whisk in the milk and bring the béchamel sauce to a simmer.

6. Reduce the heat to low. Add the cheese, shallot, Worcestershire sauce, salt, pepper, and mustard. Stir until the cheese melts, then remove from the heat.

7. Pour the sauce over the macaroni and mix well. Transfer the pasta and sauce to the greased casserole dish and sprinkle with breadcrumbs.

8. Bake, uncovered, for 30 minutes or until the top browns lightly.

9. Let the macaroni au gratin rest, covered, for 10 minutes before serving.

# MESOPOTAMIA
# HUMMUS AND PITA

"I sort of saw it all—how it used to be—the street and the houses, and he showed me ovens where they baked bread and said the Arabs used much the same kind of ovens nowadays."

—AMY LEATHERAN, *Murder in Mesopotamia*, 1936

### ⁋ YIELDS 2½ CUPS (560 GRAMS) ⁋

Inspired by the archaeological sites she visited with her second husband, archaeologist Max Mallowan, Christie set several mysteries in the Middle East, taking inspiration for her casts of characters from the academics, specialists, spouses, locals, and household staff she met there. In this mystery, Erich Leidner evokes the timelessness of the region as he explains the history of the site to nurse and narrator Amy Leatheran. With only words, he transforms the messy, dusty ruins before her into a thriving ancient village. Iraqis bake taboon bread, also called Iraqi pita, as their ancestors did in ancient times: in a communal clay oven shaped like a truncated cone. The excavation site cook's recipe would have differed little from how the people who lived there in antiquity made it. This recipe for hummus goes nicely with pita bread from your local Middle Eastern grocery store.

2 cups (340 grams) cooked or
    canned chickpeas
Juice of 2 medium lemons
½ cup (120 grams) tahini
2 garlic cloves, peeled and crushed

½ teaspoon salt
1 pinch cayenne pepper
Fresh parsley for garnish
Pita bread
Green or black olives

1. In a medium bowl, mash the chickpeas well, slowly adding ⅓ cup (80 millilitres) water and the lemon juice.

2. Stir in the tahini, garlic, salt, and cayenne pepper. Mix well.

3. Garnish with parsley and serve with pita bread and olives.

# MICHAELMAS SAGE AND ONION STUFFING

"But that dreadful Finn of mine has got himself terribly tangled up. He did some awfully clever deduction with a dish of French beans, and now he's just detected deadly poison in the sage-and-onion stuffing of the Michaelmas goose, and I've just remembered that French beans are over by Michaelmas."

—ARIADNE OLIVER, *Cards on the Table*, 1936

### ❦ SERVES 6 TO 8 ❦

Poirot attends a special bridge and dinner party hosted by the mysterious Mr. Shaitana. Four guests may have committed murder but somehow escaped justice, and four guests are sleuths. In addition to Poirot, we have Colonel Race, ex-Army and a former MI5 agent, who first appeared in *The Man in the Brown Suit*, and Superintendent Battle of Scotland Yard, who debuted in *The Secret of Chimneys*. The fourth sleuth is Ariadne Oliver, an amateur, first introduced by Christie in "The Case of the Discontented Soldier," a short story published in 1932. Widely considered Christie's literary alter ego, Mrs. Oliver often offers comic relief, frequently parodying the murder-mystery genre. Oliver's mysteries feature a vegetarian Finnish detective, Sven Hjerson, though she knows nothing of Finland or vegetarians, and she often regrets Hjerson's existence. In this novel, Oliver relates having Hjerson solve a mystery with food clues—only to realize that she flubbed the timing. Green beans are a summer crop, and the feast of St. Michael, or Michaelmas, takes place on September 29. Observers traditionally served a goose on this holiday in recognition of a legend in which an Irish prince choked to death on a goose bone. St. Patrick brought him back to life, prompting the king to order a goose sacrificed every Michaelmas to honour the holy man. Mrs. Oliver may have had a stuffing recipe like this one in mind when she puzzled over her green beans and Michaelmas goose.

2 medium yellow onions

3 stalks celery

8–10 slices day-old bread

1 tablespoon extra-virgin olive oil

¼ cup (60 grams) butter

¾ teaspoon salt

½ teaspoon ground black pepper

¼ cup (16 grams) finely chopped fresh sage

2 sprigs fresh thyme

½ teaspoon freshly ground nutmeg

Up to ½ cup (120 millilitres) chicken stock (optional)

1. Preheat the oven to 400°F (200°C).

2. Chop the onions and celery and cube the bread.

3. In a large skillet over medium heat, add the olive oil and the onions. Cook, stirring occasionally, for 4–5 minutes.

4. Add the butter, celery, salt, and pepper. Reduce heat to medium-low and cook until the onions become translucent, about 30 minutes.

5. In a large bowl, combine the cubed bread, sage, thyme, nutmeg, and onion mixture and toss well.

6. If the stuffing is going into a goose, stuff now and roast as desired. If cooking the stuffing separately, add as much stock as needed to moisten but not soak the mixture.

7. Transfer the uncooked stuffing to a 9-by-13-inch (22-by-33-centimetre) glass baking dish and cover with foil.

8. Bake for 20 minutes, uncover, and bake for 10 more minutes. Serve hot.

# GRILLED
# STEAK FRITES

"'*Pour nous, un bon bifteck*—with the fried potatoes—and a good
bottle of wine. What should we have had to drink there, I wonder?'
'Well water, I should think,' I replied with a shudder."

—HERCULE POIROT AND ARTHUR HASTINGS,
*Dumb Witness*, 1937

## ⚜ SERVES 2 ⚜

Thought lost for decades, a short story called "The Incident of the Dog's Ball"
serves as the forerunner to this novel. Christie's daughter, Rosalind Hicks, safe-
guarded a trove of papers that included this unpublished story, which literary
scholar John Curran collected for first publication in *Agatha Christie's Secret
Notebooks*. Christie dedicated *Dumb Witness* to Peter, her wire-haired terrier,
the "most faithful of friends and dearest of companions, a dog in a thousand."
Bob, the fox terrier hero of the novel, presents Poirot with an important clue
but not before Poirot questions the Tripp sisters, some very unconventional
witnesses. Ever the gourmand, Poirot recoils when Isabel Tripp, a standing
member of the Vegetarian Society, offers to share their evening meal of shred-
ded raw vegetables and brown bread with him and Hastings. The sleuths take
their leave as quickly as possible, quaking at the thought of the meal and the
possibility of drinking it with well water or, worse, nonalcoholic cider. Given
the description of lunch at the George Hotel in Market Basing—superb mutton, soggy cabbage, "dispirited" potatoes, etc.—Hastings and Poirot no doubt
returned to London for a meal, just like this one, prepared by Poirot's excellent
valet, Georges. For this deceptively simple dish, the steak must be juicy, the
fries crisp, both served hot.

Two ½-pound (225 grams) rib-eye steaks

Chips from Fish and Chips at the Seven Dials Club (page 21)

1½ tablespoons salted butter, melted

Sea salt and freshly ground black pepper

2 tablespoons (30 millilitres) herbed butter

---

1. Remove the steaks from the refrigerator 1 hour before cooking.

2. Make half the recipe (2 servings) for Chips at the Seven Dials Club, steps 1–4, and set aside.

3. Heat the grill to high.

4. Brush the steaks with the melted butter and season with salt and pepper to taste.

5. Grill the steaks for 3 minutes per side for medium rare.

6. Top each steak with 1 tablespoon herbed butter.

7. Plate the steaks, serve the fries on the side, and pair with a bottle of Cabernet Sauvignon.

# LEMON SQUASH ON THE *KARNAK*

"'You may have noticed I never drink anything but water—or perhaps lemonade. I cannot bear the taste of spirits.'

'Then may I order you a lemon squash, Madame?'"

—SALOME OTTERBOURNE AND HERCULE POIROT,
*Death on the Nile*, 1937

### ⅌ SERVES 2 ⅌

Returning once more to the Middle East, Christie sends Poirot up the Nile on the *Karnak*, a steamer ship. Affluent English and American travelers on these cruises didn't want to eat local fare. The chefs, whether Egyptian or otherwise, worked hard to make local meats, fishes, and vegetables taste familiar to passengers. Christie doesn't elaborate on the cruise's meals, but the drinking habits of her characters provide a valuable clue. Squash is a concentrated syrup made from fruit juice, water, and sugar, often mixed with alcohol or carbonated water or both before serving. On a hot summer day, enjoy this lemon squash without alcohol, as Mrs. Otterbourne claims she does, or, as Miss Marple likely would, with gin.

3 ounces (90 millilitres) gin (optional)

4 tablespoons fresh lemon juice

2 teaspoons Simple Syrup (recipe follows)

Club soda or carbonated mineral water

Lemon peel for garnish

1. In Collins glasses, add 3–4 ice cubes each and gin if using.

2. Add the lemon juice and simple syrup. Stir well and top with
   the club soda or carbonated mineral water.

3. Garnish with the lemon peel and serve with a straw.

# SIMPLE SYRUP

2 tablespoons sugar

1¼ cups (300 millilitres) water

1. In a medium saucepan over medium heat, add the sugar and water.

2. Bring to a simmer and cook for 1 minute. Remove from the heat, let cool to room temperature, and refrigerate for at least 1 hour. Keeps for up to 2 weeks.

# SEAFOOD COCKTAIL
# AT THE SAVOY

"Later, they sat around a supper table at the Savoy. . . . Nadine, sitting opposite Ginevra, said, 'How exciting it is, to be here in London with Jinny acting Ophelia and being so famous!'"

—from *Appointment with Death*, 1938

### ⅍ SERVES 4 ⅍

This archaeologically inspired mystery takes place in Jerusalem, but this recipe comes from the end of the story, when the mystery of the missing doctor's bag has been solved and when the remaining members of the Boynton family have returned to London, free from suspicion of murder and the influence of their overbearing guardian. Two icons, hotelier César Ritz and chef Auguste Escoffier, presided over the kitchens of the Savoy Hotel, transforming them from stuffy Victorian stalwarts to Edwardian stars. They served legendary dishes, including this famous king crab and prawn cocktail.

## COCKTAIL SAUCE

4 tablespoons mayonnaise

2 tablespoons ketchup

Juice of 1 large lemon

1 or 2 dashes Tabasco sauce

1 or 2 dashes Worcestershire sauce

## SEAFOOD COCKTAIL

½ small head radicchio

1 large bunch watercress

½ lemon

1 head Boston or other soft leaf lettuce

7 ounces (200 grams) white crabmeat

9 ounces (250 grams) large prawns or shrimp, cooked, peeled, and deveined

Zest of ½ medium lemon for garnish

4 pinches sweet paprika

1. First make the Cocktail Sauce. In a small bowl, mix the mayonnaise, ketchup, lemon juice, Tabasco sauce, and Worcestershire sauce together. Set aside.

2. Shred the radicchio, chop the watercress, and quarter the ½ lemon into wedges.

3. Divide the radicchio among 4 small bowls or dishes and arrange the lettuce leaves atop the radicchio.

4. Divide the crabmeat and prawns among the 4 bowls.

5. Top each with watercress, a heaping tablespoon of cocktail sauce, lemon zest, and paprika.

6. Garnish with the lemon wedges and pair with chilled Champagne.

# CHRISTMAS EVE LOBSTER SOUFFLÉ

"Tressilian went round with the soufflé. It struck him . . . that everyone was very silent tonight."

—from *Hercule Poirot's Christmas*, 1938

### ❄ SERVES 4 ❄

First appearing serially in *Collier's* magazine in America and the *Daily Express* in Britain, this classic mystery takes place in an isolated country manor house that hides plenty of secrets—including what was for dinner on Christmas Eve. For that important scene, Christie provides only one hint about the delicacies served, focusing her attention instead on the increasing tension among the characters. In 1930s England, country manor houses traditionally served a roast for Christmas Eve: a standing rib roast or a crown roast of pork paired with roasted or baked vegetables and gravy. Next came the soufflé, and for an important meal such as Christmas Eve dinner, it would have been a special soufflé, like this one made with lobster.

1 tablespoon (14 grams) unsalted butter, plus more for greasing

5 large eggs

1½ tablespoons flour

1 cup (240 millilitres) whole milk

¼ teaspoon sea salt

¼ teaspoon freshly cracked black pepper

2 tablespoons finely chopped fresh tarragon

2 cups (1 pint) cooked lobster meat

1 tablespoon heavy or whipping (double) cream

---

1. Preheat the oven to 375°F (190°C).

2. Grease a medium soufflé dish or 4 individual ones.

3. Separate the egg yolks from the whites.

4. In a medium saucepan over medium heat, melt 1 tablespoon (14 grams) butter.

5. Whisk in the flour and slowly stir in the milk, stirring constantly. Cook until the mixture thickens.

6. Reduce heat to low and whisk in the egg yolks, one at a time, until smooth.

7. Add the salt, pepper, tarragon, lobster meat, and cream. Mix well.

8. Remove the saucepan from the heat and set aside.

9. With a hand mixer or immersion blender, beat the egg whites until stiff.

10. Gently fold ⅓ of the egg whites into the lobster mixture until just combined.

11. Fold the lobster mixture into the remaining egg whites until just combined.

12. Pour the mixture into the greased dish and bake for 20–25 minutes or individual dishes for 12–15 minutes, until the top puffs and browns with a set center.

13. Serve immediately and pair with a bottle of Chablis.

# DERBY DAY STRAWBERRIES AND CREAM

"'Then I suppose you didn't go to the Derby?'
'No, indeed.'
'Anybody go to it from here?'
'Major Horton did. He's quite a keen racing man. And Mr. Abbot usually takes the day off. He didn't back the winner, though.'"

—LUKE FITZWILLIAM AND MR. JONES,
*Murder Is Easy,* 1939

### ❧ SERVES 8 ❧

Thomas Wolsey, lord high chancellor of England during the reign of King Henry VIII, receives credit for first serving strawberries—wild and smaller than the garden variety we know today—with cream. Epsom's earliest horse races may have run before the English Civil War, but the first derby occurred in 1780. The race's name purportedly came from a coin toss between Edward Smith-Stanley, 12th Earl of Derby, and Sir Charles Bunbury. Derby apparently won, though no solid evidence supports the tale. Races on Epsom Downs became a regular feature of the sporting season, and the local gentry provided the cups, plates, and guineas for the derby while the Surrey countryside provided the strawberries and cream. From then on, people of means flocked to Epsom for a sporting day out. Set in the fictional village of Wychwood under Ashe, near Epsom Downs, this mystery has it all: an obnoxious lord, a hint of black magic, several spinsters, a retired colonel, and a strange series of accidents, the latest of which happens on Derby Day, when a local woman is murdered in London. Racegoers then and now celebrate one of Britain's most prestigious races with strawberries and cream, a simple, elegant dish perfectly at odds with murder. The cream in question can take one or more of three forms: liquid heavy cream poured over the berries, heavy cream whipped and dolloped atop the fruit, or crème fraîche spooned on them.

6 cups (1 kilogram) strawberries

2 tablespoons granulated white sugar

1 cup (240 millilitres) heavy (double) cream (optional)

2 cups (470 millilitres) whipped cream (optional)

1 cup (240 millilitres) crème fraîche (optional)

---

1. Bring the strawberries to room temperature, hull them, and halve them.

2. In a large bowl, add the strawberries, sprinkle them with the sugar, and stir to coat them evenly.

3. Divide the sugared berries into 8 dessert cups.

4. Pour the heavy (double) cream, dollop the whipped cream, or top with crème fraîche and serve immediately.

# DEVON BOILED POTATOES

"I hope lunch will be satisfactory. There is cold ham and cold tongue, and I've boiled some potatoes."

—THOMAS ROGERS, *And Then There Were None*, 1939

### ❧ SERVES 4 ❧

Christie claimed that this novel was the hardest for her to write. It became her best-selling novel and the best-selling mystery of all time, with more than 100 million copies sold. Most critics and fans consider it her masterpiece. An unknown host lures 10 strangers to an island off the coast of Devon, and the deteriorating quality of their meals heightens the tension. At first, the food and drink provide goodwill: "The food had been good, the wine perfect. . . . Everyone was in better spirits." But after two of the guests die, meals decline in sustenance and goodwill. ("Eight little Soldier Boys travelling in Devon; / One said he'd stay there, and then there were seven.") By the time half of the guests have died, the survivors meet in the kitchen and eat from tins, standing up. Boiled potatoes lie exactly halfway between comfort food and bare bones. Use whole potatoes of the same size so they cook evenly.

**1 pound (450 grams) small potatoes**

**½ teaspoon sea salt**

**2 tablespoons unsalted butter, melted**

1. In a large pot over medium heat, add the potatoes and cover them with cold water by 1 inch (2.5 centimetres).

2. Add half the salt and bring to a boil. Cook, uncovered, until tender, about 8–15 minutes. If too much water boils off, add a little more.

3. After 8 minutes, poke the potatoes with a skewer. When it moves easily through the center, they're done.

4. Drain the potatoes and place in a serving bowl.

5. Drizzle the potatoes with the melted butter, season with the remaining salt, toss gently, and serve.

1940s

W AR once more set fire to the world, casting a blood-soaked shadow over the first half of the decade. The destruction of agriculture and international trade affected everyone. Amid shortages and rations, households had to survive on meals made with as few ingredients as possible. Meat, cheese, and sugar in particular became scarce. Inventive by necessity, people reworked old recipes and created new ones with less. Butlers became increasingly rare, but cooks and maids still had work, albeit in reduced numbers.

Christie wrote her first three mysteries of the decade before World War II began. But two of the books reflect the darkening mood. *Sad Cypress* takes place during a murder trial, and *One, Two, Buckle My Shoe*, a political study of prewar society, sees Poirot dine with peaceniks, fascists, and bankers. For the third novel of the decade, *Evil under the Sun,* Christie turns to escapism. On holiday, like Christie when she wrote it, Poirot enjoys chocolate and fruity cocktails.

Now in her 50s, Christie focuses on themes of the past and remembrance. A suspect in *Murder in Retrospect* reflects on a memorable breakfast. The very Victorian Miss Barton serves proper, traditional tea in *The Moving Finger*. Other dishes in the novels of the decade look to the past as well. Kings George III and IV loved Windsor Soup, which features in *Taken at the Flood*, and the rice pilaf in *Crooked House* hails from Aristide Leonides's past. In the latter two novels, the war has ended, but its effects linger. So many people, places, and comforts lay dead, destroyed, or missing. Along with the rest of the world, Christie's characters cope with extended rationing and enduring uncertainty.

Even Christie herself didn't escape wartime scrutiny. Recently uncovered documents reveal that MI5 investigated her. In *N or M?*, published in 1941, she named one of the characters Major Bletchley. For military intelligence personnel, that name hit uncomfortably close to Bletchley Park, Britain's top-secret code-breaking center, making officials understandably suspicious.

# CRAB AND SALMON SANDWICHES

"One used to be rather afraid of eating fish pastes. There have been cases of ptomaine poisoning from them, haven't there?"

—ELINOR CARLISLE, *Sad Cypress*, 1940

### ⅗ SERVES 4 ⅗

Amid growing unease, characters become increasingly suspicious of one another. Even sharing a simple meal with a neighbour rattles nerves, and of course death calls Poirot to action. Mr. Abbott, the local grocer, assists Elinor Carlisle, the new mistress of Hunterbury, offering her the best of his tinned sandwich fillings: salmon and shrimp, turkey and tongue, salmon and sardine, or maybe ham and tongue. But her casual remark to the grocer unwittingly sows the seeds for gossip and rumour. Miss Carlisle invites her romantic rival, Mary Gerrard, and the district nurse for a light, impromptu lunch of sandwiches and tea. Did Miss Carlisle poison her neighbour, was it a case of badly tinned sandwich paste, or is the air of paranoia intentionally creating a red herring? Suspicion of tinned foods and the assumption of food poisoning from unfamiliar food sources brings together the themes of fear abroad and at home. In the United Kingdom at this time, tinned food caused only one recorded case of ptomaine poisoning, but it was tinned seafood. At Hunterbury, Mrs. Bishop, the housekeeper, would have made the sandwiches for tea from scratch and with her own fresh bread. No questionable tins on her watch!

*continues*

½ pound (225 grams) cooked crabmeat

½ pound (225 grams) cooked salmon, flaked

¼ cup (15 grams) finely chopped shallot

2 tablespoons mayonnaise

1 tablespoon finely chopped fresh tarragon

1 tablespoon fresh lemon juice

½ teaspoon Worcestershire sauce

¼ teaspoon salt

Fresh bread

Edible flower or watercress for garnish

1. In a food processor, combine the crab, salmon, shallot, mayonnaise, tarragon, lemon juice, Worcestershire sauce, and salt. Pulse to a paste and refrigerate, covered, until ready to serve.

2. When ready to serve, spread the paste between slices of fresh bread.

3. Trim all crusts, then cut the sandwiches into small triangles or squares. Plate the sandwiches and garnish with an edible flower or watercress.

4. If served midafternoon, pair the sandwiches, as Mrs. Bishop would, with a pot of Darjeeling tea.

# GRILLED DOVER SOLE

"The wines at dinner stirred Poirot to a passion of appreciation. They had a perfect clear soup, a grilled sole, saddle of lamb with tiny young garden peas and strawberries and cream."

—from *One, Two, Buckle My Shoe*, 1940

## ⅜ SERVES 4 ⅜

Christie's most political novel takes Poirot on a dining odyssey in which he meets characters of widely differing viewpoints. First, he encounters an idealist in a coffeehouse, a fitting location. The first cafés opened in 1652, and people quickly used them as meeting places to share ideas and information. After the Restoration, King Charles II so worried that anyone could go to a coffeehouse and discuss politics freely that he tried to outlaw the establishments altogether. Next, Poirot invites an earnest dental assistant and her fascist boyfriend to Sunday lunch at a local inn. Perhaps he thinks the young man, feeling uncomfortable in this middle-class setting, will talk too much. Lastly, Poirot joins a conservative banker at his country manor house for a traditional Sunday dinner. The sleuth approves of the host's good taste and fine hospitality. The best English dishes usually are the simplest ones, and this is a simple recipe for one of the best English fishes. Dover sole has crisp, white flesh, firm to the touch, and tastes almost sweet. Freshness is paramount.

*continues*

**Four 7-ounce (200 grams) Dover soles, cleaned and skinned**

**½ cup (60 grams) all-purpose (white) flour**

**Salt and pepper**

**2⅓ tablespoons unsalted butter**

**Chopped fresh parsley**

**Lemon slices (optional)**

---

1. Remove the fish from the refrigerator 1 hour before cooking. If they need cleaning and skinning, do so now.

2. Preheat the oven to 350°F (180°C) or heat the grill to high.

3. On a sheet of wax paper, sprinkle the flour and dust each fish on both sides. Season with salt and pepper to taste.

4. If using the oven, line a baking sheet with aluminum foil and lay the fish on it. On a char-grill, lay the fish directly on the grill.

5. In a small pan over medium heat, melt 2 tablespoons butter and stir in parsley to taste.

6. Brush the herbed butter on the fish and grill or bake for 4–5 minutes.

7. Carefully turn the fish over, brush them with the remaining 1 teaspoon of butter, and grill or bake for 4–5 more minutes.

8. Warm a serving dish, plate the fish on it, and spoon any cooking juices from the baking sheet onto the fish.

9. Garnish with fresh parsley and lemon slices if desired.

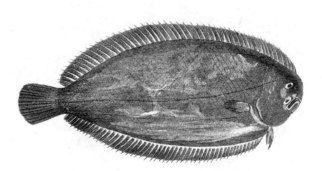

# JOLLY ROGER
# COCKTAIL

"It was enlarged and improved in 1934 by the addition of a cocktail bar,
a bigger dining-room and some extra bathrooms. The prices
went up. People said: 'Ever been to Leathercombe Bay? Awfully jolly
hotel there, on a sort of island.'"

—from *Evil under the Sun*, 1941

## ⚜ YIELDS 1 COCKTAIL ⚜

The setting for this holiday mystery takes inspiration from the hotel on Burgh
Island, a tidal island off the coast of South Devon. In 1927, George Chirgwin,
a music hall star, sold Burgh Island to filmmaker Archibald Nettlefold, who
built a stunning art deco hotel there. The island became one of the most popular hotels of the 1930s. Christie frequently visited, and the hotel built Beach
House, an adjacent cottage, in the 1930s as a writer's retreat for her. Improve-
ments included the addition of a cocktail bar called the Captain's Cabin, literally the captain's cabin from a ship. In England's growing seaside towns, where
Poirot is holidaying, the aristocracy built summer homes, the wealthy stayed in
grand hotels, and nearby working-class families brought picnics to the beach.
On warm, sunny days, buses and trains soon brought even more bodies to the
beaches. Legend has it that pirates invented this cocktail to prevent scurvy,
but at the seaside during holiday season, a Jolly Roger or two prevents sobriety.

*continues*

**1 ounce (30 millilitres) dark rum**

**1 ounce (30 millilitres) Galliano or ½ ounce (15 millilitres) Grand Marnier**

**½ ounce (15 millilitres) apricot brandy**

**3 ounces (90 millilitres) orange juice**

**Apricot, orange, and kiwifruit for garnish**

1. In a cocktail shaker filled with ice, add all the liquids. Shake well for 30 seconds.

2. Strain into a collins glass and garnish with slices of apricot, orange, and kiwifruit.

# FIFTH COLUMN
# BLACKBERRY JAM

> "'Have you been a good girl, Betty?'
> To which Betty replied laconically by the single word:
> 'Dam!'
> This, however, was not to be regarded as an expression of
> disapproval at her mother's return, but merely as a request for
> blackberry preserve."

—MRS. SPROT AND BETTY SPROT, *N or M?*, 1941

### ❦ YIELDS 1 PINT (300 GRAMS) ❦

During the war, Christie rarely mentions the elaborate meals that played such an important role in the previous two decades. Dinners shared by Tommy and Tuppence Beresford, who once indulged at the Savoy and other luxury hotels, have grown boring, predictable, and impossibly governed by rationing. The excitement of a spy mission no doubt whetted their appetites.

Tommy Beresford is looking for Fifth Column spies in Leahampton, a fictional seaside town on the south coast of England, where Mrs. Perenna runs her Sans Souci hotel. Meals there likely come from the sea, local gardens, and a bit of black market. Betty Sprot, the toddler heroine of the novel, expresses an appreciation for the sweeter side of the spoon by replying to all questions with a request for her favourite fruit spread. In honour of Betty's alarming locution, here's a recipe for jam made from berries found at the end of any lane. They're "Dam!" good.

*continues*

**3 cups (450 grams) fresh
  blackberries**

**1¼ cups (250 grams) granulated
  white sugar**

**¼ teaspoon lemon juice**

**1 pinch salt**

1. In a medium pot, mash the blackberries.

2. Add the sugar, lemon juice, and salt and stir well.

3. Place the pot over medium heat, stirring gently, until the sugar dissolves.

4. Increase the heat to medium-high and boil the mixture, stirring frequently, for 10 minutes.

5. Pour the jam into a jam jar and close the lid tightly. Allow to cool to room temperature before refrigerating. In the fridge, it will keep for several weeks.

# ORANGE MARMALADE FROM GOSSINGTON HALL

"Hastily downing the last fragments of toast and marmalade with a drink of coffee, Colonel Bantry hurried out into the hall and was relieved to see Colonel Melchett, the chief constable of the county."

—from *The Body in the Library*, 1942

### ❧ YIELDS 1 SMALL JAR (300 GRAMS) ❧

This classic mystery begins at Gossington Hall, the manor house in St. Mary Mead, in which a housemaid's declaration of a body in the library wakes Dolly Bantry. Not believing such an unlikely tale, Mrs. Bantry sends her husband, Arthur, to investigate. Unfortunately, the colonel finds truth in the announcement: a dead girl in an evening dress on a bearskin rug in the library. Neither the girl nor the rug belongs to the Bantrys. Colonel Bantry munches on breakfast while waiting for the police to arrive. Meanwhile, Mrs. Bantry has called Jane Marple, friend and neighbour, to investigate. The marmalade on which the colonel munches would have come from orange trees in the house's orangerie. Typically made from oranges grown in dedicated greenhouses, orange marmalade was one of the most common toast toppings in Britain at this time. In the 900s, Moors brought oranges, native to southeast Asia, to Spain. From there, the bitter fruits spread across the Mediterranean. Food lore claims that they first became marmalade when a Spanish ship full of them broke down in the port of Dundee and resourceful Scots cooked the fruit into a delicious spread that

*continues*

eventually made its way to Colonel Bantry's breakfast table. Seville oranges, available only from the end of December to mid-February, are the key to this recipe. Other oranges taste too sweet, so no substitutions!

3 Seville oranges

1 cup (200 grams) granulated white sugar

1. Wash the fruit well and zest half of 1 orange.

2. Peel the zested orange and the other 2 oranges. Reserve the peel from 1 orange and slice it into thin slivers.

3. Squeeze the peeled oranges, reserving the pulp and juice and discarding the pith and seeds.

4. In a thick-bottomed pan over medium heat, add the pulp, juice, zest, slivers of peel, and 1½ cups (360 millilitres) water. Bring to a boil, stirring regularly.

5. Reduce the heat to medium-low and simmer, uncovered, for 30 minutes.

6. Slowly add the sugar, stirring until it dissolves.

7. Simmer for 20 more minutes, stirring regularly until the marmalade thickens.

8. Pour or ladle the marmalade into a sterilized jam jar. Let it cool to room temperature before refrigerating. It will keep for several weeks in the fridge.

# DEVILED LAMB KIDNEYS

"Funny, the things you do remember. I remember the taste of the kidneys and bacon I ate quite well. They were very good kidneys. Devilled."

—PHILIP BLAKE, *Five Little Pigs*, 1942

### ❧ SERVES 2 ❧

Investigating a murder always proves challenging, but especially 16 years after the event. The daughter of famous painter Amyas Crale asks Poirot to investigate her father's murder. She believes that her mother, who died in prison, was convicted wrongly for it. As Poirot discovers, all five people closest to the crime remember matters differently. When it happened, the suspects were eating lunch together while the victim was painting and sipping questionable beer. Philip Blake, Crale's best friend, pens an account of the morning of the murder, recalling coming down late for breakfast and finding no one in the dining room. But he does remember these deviled kidneys, a Victorian breakfast dish in which lamb kidneys cook in a spicy sauce before going on toast. In the Edwardian era, gentlemen's clubs and country homes often served this popular meal. Deviling, though it sounds sinister, entails preparing any food with Worcestershire sauce, cayenne pepper, mustard, salt, pepper, and butter.

*continues*

4 lamb kidneys

1 tablespoon (14 grams) unsalted butter

2 ounces (60 millilitres) dry Sherry

1 tablespoon white wine or apple cider vinegar

1 teaspoon red currant jelly

Worcestershire sauce

1 pinch cayenne pepper

1 teaspoon dry English mustard

1 tablespoon heavy (double) cream

Salt and pepper

Chopped parsley for garnish

Fried bread from A Full English at Nasse House (page 117)

---

1. Quarter the kidneys or cut them into ½-inch (1-centimetre) slices.

2. In a small frying pan over medium heat, melt the butter. Add the kidneys and cook for 1 minute.

3. Turn the kidneys over and cook for 1 more minute, until both sides have browned.

4. Add the Sherry and let it bubble, then add the vinegar and jelly, stirring to dissolve.

5. Mix in the Worcestershire sauce to taste, the cayenne pepper, and dry mustard.

6. Reduce the heat to medium-low and stir in the cream. Simmer, uncovered, for 1–2 minutes, until the sauce has reduced and looks glossy.

7. Season with salt and pepper to taste.

8. Garnish with parsley and serve on fried bread.

---

**NOTE:** *You can substitute apple or grape jelly for the red currant jelly.*

# A PERFECT
# CUP OF TEA

"Florence came in bearing a tray of tea with some fine Crown Derby cups on it, which I gather Miss Emily had brought with her. The tea was China and delicious and there were plates of sandwiches and thin bread and butter, and a quantity of little cakes."

—JERRY BURTON, *The Moving Finger*, 1942

## ⚜ YIELDS 2 CUPS ⚜

In a village still coping with the aftermath of war, Emily Barton—a charming Victorian spinster and the last of the Barton family—finds herself in financial trouble. Miss Barton turns to Florence, her former parlor maid, for help. Ever loyal, Florence finds room for her former mistress in her new home, and Miss Barton rents out her family home to recovering veteran Jerry Burton and his sister, Joanna. The Burton siblings visit Miss Barton, and Florence serves an excellent, traditional tea, just as she made for the Barton sisters every day for decades. European merchants and missionaries brought tea from China, where boiling water poured over fresh or dried leaves of *Camellia sinensis* originally served as a medicinal tonic. Traded around the world for centuries by the Chinese, Japanese, Dutch, and English, tea now grows around the world, from Australia and Iran to Mozambique and Peru. It has become the most consumed beverage on earth, after water, and today it plays a vital role in many cultures and social practices, including Japanese tea ceremonies, Arabic tea gatherings, and of course British afternoon tea.

*continues*

**2 teaspoons loose black or white tea or 2 teabags**

**Whole milk (optional)**

**Granulated white or brown sugar (optional)**

**Honey (optional)**

**1 lemon (optional)**

---

1. Set a kettle filled with 2 cups (500 millilitres) of filtered water over medium-high heat to boil.

2. For white tea, let the water cool for about 30 seconds to approximately 160°F (70°C). For black tea, use water at a rolling boil.

3. Preheat the teapot by adding a little water from the kettle and cover the pot with the lid. Let the teapot warm, about 1 minute, then pour the water out. Return the kettle to the heat if the water has cooled too much.

4. If using loose tea, place leaves into an infuser or add them directly to the teapot and use a tea strainer when pouring. If using teabags, place them in the teapot.

5. Add 2 cups of the hot or boiling water to the teapot, pouring over the tea leaves or tea bags directly, replace the lid, and cover the teapot with a cozy to retain the heat. Some white teas need to steep for as little as 1 minute; others require more time. Most black teas need 3–5 minutes.

6. If using milk, add the desired amount to the cups before the tea.

7. Remove the infuser or tea bags, if using, and pour into cups. Pour loose-leaf tea through a tea strainer.

8. Serve with sugar, honey, and/or lemon.

# BEETROOT AND WATERCRESS SALAD

"Mr. Treves sipped his glass of port appreciatively. A very nice wine.
And an excellently cooked and served dinner."

—from *Towards Zero*, 1944

### ⁂ SERVES 8 ⁂

Lady Tressilian may be bed-ridden, but family and friends stay and dine all
season long at Gull's Point, her home on the south coast of England. Nevile
Strange, a tennis star and her husband's former ward; Strange's wife, Kay; his
ex-wife, Audrey; and Thomas, an old friend of the family, are staying as guests
in the house. Mr. Treves, an elderly barrister who has brought an introduction
from a mutual friend of Lady Tressilian, and Ted, a friend of Kay Strange, are
staying in nearby hotels but come to Gull's Point for dinner. Mary Aldin, Lady
Tressilian's distant cousin and companion, serves as hostess for the dinner. In
a seaside country house, dinner had fewer courses in the early 1940s than in
previous decades, but, like the dinner served at End House a decade earlier, it
featured local food, including fish and vegetables grown in kitchen gardens.
Throughout the war, people regularly ate beets and watercress, both widely
available in Britain, and the salad has become popular once again.

*continues*

| | |
|---|---|
| **4 beets** | **Salt and pepper** |
| **2 tablespoons extra-virgin olive oil** | **1 bunch watercress, thick stalks removed** |
| **1 tablespoon honey** | |

---

1. Clean the beets thoroughly but don't prick or break the skin or they'll lose their color.

2. In a large pot of water over medium-high heat, add the beets, cover them completely with water, and bring to a boil.

3. Reduce the heat to medium-low and simmer until tender, about 45–60 minutes. Make sure that liquid covers the beets at all times. To check for doneness, use a slotted spoon to remove a beet from the pot and poke it with a skewer or toothpick. They're done when the skewer or toothpick moves easily through the flesh to the center.

4. Drain the beets and let them cool.

5. Under cold water, rub off the skins and discard.

6. Cut the peeled beets into ¼-inch (1-centimetre) slices.

7. In a small bowl, whisk together the oil, honey, and salt and pepper to taste.

8. Place the watercress in a salad bowl, pour on the dressing, and toss.

9. To serve, divide the dressed watercress among 8 salad plates and top with the sliced beets.

# TIGER NUT SWEETS

"No, no, my little one, do not eat your doll's hair. See, here is
something better—a sweet—oh, how good."

—KAIT, *Death Comes as the End*, 1944

## ⁘ YIELDS 24 BALLS ⁘

With this novel—set in Thebes, Egypt, in 2000 B.C.—Christie established a
new genre: the historical whodunit. She took inspiration from letters written
during the Middle Kingdom by a man complaining to his family about their
treatment of his concubine. Farmers of this era grew emmer, a kind of wheat,
for bread and barley for beer, the two biggest cash crops of ancient Egypt.
Most farms also had small kitchen gardens that grew cabbages, dates, figs,
leeks, lentils, onions, and other foods. Farmers bought meat and fish from local
hunters and fishermen. In Christie's time, wealthy prewar farmers lived a not
dissimilar lifestyle. In the kitchens, women prepared food, laughed, scolded one
another, and minded their children. This mystery follows Renisenb, a young
widow who has returned to her wealthy father's farm with her child. In this
scene, Renisenb's sister-in-law, Kait, offers a child a sweet. Here is a recipe for
an ancient treat made from dates and honey that tastes deliciously aromatic.

2 cups (340 grams) fresh dates,
    pitted
2 tablespoons ground cinnamon
½ teaspoon cardamom powder
¼ cup (32 grams) coarsely chopped
    walnuts

2 tablespoons honey
½ cup (75 grams) finely chopped
    blanched almonds

*continues*

1. In a food processor, combine the dates, cinnamon, cardamom, and walnuts. Pulse, adding 1 tablespoon of water at a time, until a paste forms.

2. Transfer the mixture to a bowl and refrigerate for 30 minutes.

3. Roll 1 heaping tablespoon of the mixture into a ball and place on a plate. Repeat with the rest of the mixture.

4. Line a large baking sheet with parchment or waxed paper, pour the honey into a shallow bowl, and pour the almond bits into another shallow bowl or plate.

5. Roll the balls first in honey, then in the almonds, until covered. Place them on the paper to rest for 1 hour before eating.

6. Store in an airtight container and refrigerate up to 1 week.

# CHAMPAGNE OYSTERS AT THE HOTEL LUXEMBOURG

"'Tell me about the champagne.'
'It was Clicquot, 1928—very good and expensive wine. Mr.
Barton was like that—he like good food and drink—the best.'"

—JOHNNIE RACE AND GIUSEPPE,
*Sparkling Cyanide*, 1945

#### ❦ SERVES 8 ❦

This stand-alone mystery begins at a dinner party at the Hotel Luxembourg, a lavish establishment much like the Savoy, Ritz, or Dorchester. Built in the 1880s, the Savoy, Britain's first luxury hotel, introduced indoor electric lights, lifts, and running water in the bathrooms. César Ritz, the first and most famous chef at the Savoy, opened his eponymous hotel in 1906. The Dorchester opened in the 1930s and, like its predecessors, also survived the war beautifully intact. At the fictional Luxembourg, the deaths of a woman and her husband occur precisely one year apart in the same place with the same dinner-party guests. We don't know what courses the hotel served at either ill-fated gathering, but where there's Champagne, you often will find oysters.

*continues*

32 fresh oysters

2 cups (500 millilitres) Champagne

½ teaspoon chopped flat parsley

½ teaspoon fresh chopped tarragon

½ teaspoon dry mustard

1 tablespoon black peppercorns

1 lemon

1 cup (30 grams) spinach leaves, washed and chopped

2 tablespoons scallions, thinly sliced

¼ cup (40 grams) sweet red peppers, thinly sliced

1 tablespoon clarified butter

Sea salt and freshly ground black pepper

---

1. With a shucking knife, open the oysters and cut the meat from the shells into a small bowl. Discard the flatter top shells and reserve the deeper bottom shells. Set aside.

2. In a large frying pan over high heat, combine the oysters, Champagne, parsley, tarragon, mustard, and peppercorns and poach for 1 minute.

3. While the oysters are poaching, place the reserved shells on a serving platter.

4. With tongs or a slotted spoon, remove the oysters from the pan and place them back in the plated shells.

5. Reduce the heat to medium and reduce the poaching liquid by half.

6. While reducing the poaching liquid, zest the lemon and juice it. Set aside.

7. Spoon the poaching liquid over the oysters.

8.  In another pan over medium-low heat, sauté the spinach, scallions, lemon zest, and peppers in the clarified butter for 1 minute.

9.  Plate the sautéed vegetables with the oysters.

10. Deglaze the second frying pan with the lemon juice seasoned with sea salt and freshly ground pepper to taste.

11. Pour the lemon juice mixture over the oysters and vegetables, serve warm, and pair with a bottle of Veuve Clicquot.

# CARAMEL CUSTARD

"We are only, as she knows, moderately fond of caramel custard. There
would be something very gross, just after the death of a friend,
in eating one's favorite pudding."

—LUCY ANGKATELL, *The Hollow*, 1946

### ❦ SERVES 8 ❦

In this country-house murder, a possible murder weapon hides in a basket of
fresh eggs, and Christie cleverly draws her characters using the experiences of
two women serving meals in different social situations. For Gerda Christow,
a middle-class doctor's wife, preparing lunch for her husband creates con-
stant anxiety. Is it better to suffer his disapproval if lunch cools or to have him
arrive just after she has sent it back to the kitchen to keep warm? For Lucy
Angkatell, hostess for a weekend party at The Hollow, food serves as a social
statement. She worries most about the awkwardness of having roast duck for
lunch shortly after the murder of a guest. It comes as a great relief when her
butler announces sandwiches and coffee in the dining room and even more
of a relief when Mrs. Medway, the cook, prepares a simple caramel custard
for pudding. In Britain, pudding is an alternate name for the dessert course,
regardless of whether the dish itself consists of cake, pudding, or fruit and
cream. It also can taste savoury and serve as a side dish to the main course,
such as Yorkshire pudding.

1¾ cup (350 grams) superfine
  (caster) sugar

6 large fresh eggs

1 teaspoon vanilla extract

1¼ cups (300 millilitres) heavy
  cream (double cream)

1¼ cups (300 millilitres) whole
  milk

1. Preheat the oven to 350°F (180°C).

2. In a small pot over low heat, combine ¾ cup (150 grams) sugar and ½ cup (120 millilitres) water. Stir continuously until the sugar dissolves and the mixture starts to boil.

3. Boil, uncovered, until the mixture achieves a deep caramel color. Remove from the heat and let the bubbles subside.

4. Pour the caramel syrup into a deep 8-inch (20-centimetre) round cake pan. Allow to cool to room temperature.

5. Meanwhile, in a large bowl, whisk together the eggs, vanilla extract, and the remaining 1 cup (200 grams) of sugar. Whisk well but stop before it becomes foamy.

6. In a medium pot over medium heat, add the cream and milk and bring to a boil. At the same time, set a kettle filled with 2–4 cups (0.5–1 litre) of water over high heat to boil.

7. Remove the cream mixture from the heat and, whisking continuously, pour it into the egg mixture in the large bowl. Stir to combine.

8. Pour the combined mixture into the cake pan, using a strainer to remove any clumpy bits.

9. Place the cake pan in a larger, deep baking pan and add the boiling water into the outer pan until the water reaches halfway up the side of the cake pan.

10. Carefully place the cake pan in the oven and bake for 40 minutes or until set.

11. Toothpick-test for doneness and allow to cool if serving warm.

12. If serving chilled, allow to cool to room temperature, cover, and refrigerate overnight.

13. To remove the custard from the cake pan, slide a butter knife around the outside edge, cover with a serving plate, and carefully turn over.

# FRESH
# WINDSOR SOUP

"Poirot knew well that . . . small cups of a treacly and muddy
liquid called Black Coffee were served not in the Coffee-Room but in
the lounge. The Windsor Soup, Vienna Steak and Potatoes,
and Steamed Pudding which comprised Dinner would be obtainable
in the Coffee-Room at seven sharp."

—from *Taken at the Flood*, 1948

## ❦ SERVES 4 ❦

The Cloades, a typical extended family living in Warmsley Vale, a village not far from London, stand in for all Britons recovering mentally and physically from the bloody conflict of World War II. Food shortages and rationing continued years after the Axis powers surrendered, and pub meals proved particularly bland. The British diet had changed drastically and not always for the better. The Stag, the country pub and hotel at which Poirot stays to solve this mystery, exhibits typical period indifference to guests in terms of service and cuisine. Windsor Soup, purportedly a favourite of kings George III and IV, appeared often in cookbooks published during Queen Victoria's reign. But the drab, postwar version sold in tins or served in pubs and lunchrooms gave the dish a bad name. When made properly at home, with fresh ingredients, spices, and wine, Poirot enjoys this delicious stew.

¼ pound (110 grams) stewing beef

¼ pound (110 grams) lamb

1 medium yellow onion

1 large carrot

1 large parsnip

2 tablespoons bleached all-purpose (white) flour

2 tablespoons salted butter

4 cups (1 litre) beef stock

1 bouquet garni (parsley, thyme, bay leaf, and a few peppercorns tied together in a leek leaf or cheesecloth with twine)

½ teaspoon chili powder

Salt and pepper

¼ cup (60 millilitres) Madeira wine (optional)

---

1. Cube the beef and lamb, coarsely chop the onion, and peel and slice the carrot and parsnip into ¼-inch (6-millimetre) rounds.

2. Lightly coat the meat cubes with flour. Reserve the remaining flour.

3. In a large pot over medium heat, melt the butter. Add the meat and brown it for about 3 minutes.

4. Add the remaining flour and cook for 1–2 more minutes.

5. Add the onions, carrots, and parsnips and sauté for 1–2 minutes.

6. Stir in the stock and add the bouquet garni, chili powder, and salt and pepper to taste.

7. Simmer over medium-low heat, uncovered, for at least 2 hours, stirring occasionally.

8. With a fork or slotted spoon, carefully remove the bouquet garni. Stir and season to taste.

9. Divide the soup among 4 bowls. If using, add 1 tablespoon (15 millilitres) of Madeira to each bowl.

10. Serve with crusty bread and pair with a hearty white wine, such as a white Bordeaux.

# GREEK RICE PILAF

"He gave me a free hand—I will say that. Nurses, governesses, schools.
And proper wholesome nursery food—not those queer spiced rice
dishes he used to eat."

—EDITH DE HAVILAND, *Crooked House*, 1949

### ❧ SERVES 6-8 ❧

Set in postwar London, this mystery features the extended family of Aristide
Leonides, a Greek from Smyrna who arrived in England in 1884, age 24 and
penniless. Leonides becomes a successful businessman and marries an upper-
class Englishwoman, living in a huge suburban home outside London. But even
after all his successes, he comes from a different place with a different language
and different tastes than the rest of his English family. His adopted country,
while venerating the Elgin Marbles, still considers him an outsider, as does
his own family. Red herrings, the original mystery food, abound in this novel,
but Christie uses food to reveal Leonides's character and great-aunt Edith's
decidedly insular beliefs. Traditional Greek rice pilaf (gastronomically and
etymologically related to Spain's paella) consists of rice cooked in broth with
spices, vegetables, and meat and finished with lemon juice and feta cheese—a
hearty, ancient dish that the Leonides children might have enjoyed.

1–2 tablespoons olive oil

1 small red onion, roughly chopped

2 tablespoons butter

1½ cups (315 grams) long grain or
  basmati rice

1½ cups (360 millilitres) chicken
  broth

2 tablespoons orzo pasta

Juice of 1 lemon

Salt and freshly ground black
  pepper

Chopped parsley

⅓ cup (55 grams) feta cheese

1. In a large pan over medium heat, add the olive oil and onions and sauté, covered, until the onions soften, about 5–6 minutes.

2. Add the butter and rice and sauté, uncovered, until the rice becomes translucent, about 6–8 minutes.

3. Pour in the broth, orzo, and lemon juice to deglaze the pan. Season with salt and pepper to taste.

4. Cover, reduce the heat to medium-low, and simmer for about 15 minutes, until the rice has cooked and absorbed all the liquid. Add a little extra water if needed.

5. Stir in parsley to taste and the feta cheese.

6. Pair with a good ouzo.

1950s

EVEN though the immediate horrors of war were receding, hardships, shortages, and black markets still shaped this decade. Sugar rationing ended in 1953 and meat rationing only in 1954. *A Murder Is Announced*, Christie's first mystery of the 1950s, explores the black markets that had arisen in English villages. Britain had lost so much: lives, homes, businesses, and even records. In the 1950s, familiar comfort foods regained popularity in a changing, challenging world. *After the Funeral* features a family sustaining many losses: the death of the family patriarch, many of his brothers and sisters, and his son and heir, but the meal served after the funeral follows long-held traditional practice. *Dead Man's Folly* begins with the sad tale of a woman who lost both sons in the war, sold the ancestral estate to a wealthy stranger, and now lives in a cottage on the grounds. But the breakfast buffet at the estate could have been served anytime in the preceding century. *Ordeal by Innocence* features children adopted from London during the war who lost their families and their way of life.

The loss of official records in particular meant that people could reinvent themselves at will. Few characters in *A Murder Is Announced* are what they seem, and in *Mrs. McGinty's Dead*, the mystery that brings Poirot to a country estate run poorly as a guesthouse centers on a "Where are they now?' article in the Sunday paper. Mrs. McGinty herself works as a daily maid for the middle-class residents of the village. By this decade, only the wealthy have live-in servants. *Cat among the Pigeons* combines the loss of a Middle Eastern kingdom and characters hiding their wartime pasts. Christie herself attained a new identity in 1956, when she became a Dame Commander of the Most Excellent Order of the British Empire (DBE), which granted her the title of dame.

In 1952, *The Mousetrap*, Christie's whodunit play, premiered at the Theatre Royal in Nottingham. The decade also heralded the Cold War, political conspiracies, new music, and immigration, all of them infusing Christie's plots. *They Came to Baghdad* and *Destination Unknown* feature protagonists who explore this new world from London to the souks of Iraq and Morocco. In *Hickory Dickory Dock*, young students from all over the world come to London, ready to learn and bringing new ideas and cuisines to share. These three novels feature traditional comfort dishes that aren't British: a Middle-Eastern turkey stuffing, mint tea from Morocco, and spaghetti with meatballs by way of America and Italy.

# ANOTHER DELICIOUS DEATH BY CAKE

"'He called it Delicious Death. My cake! I will not have my cake called that!'

'It was a compliment really,' said Miss Blacklock. 'He meant it was worth dying to eat such a cake.'"

—MITZI AND LETITIA BLACKLOCK,
*A Murder Is Announced*, 1950

## ❧ YIELDS TWO 9-INCH (22-CENTIMETRE) ROUND CAKES ❧

Before World War II, Britain imported about 70 percent of its food, but Nazi blockades severely disrupted this trade and created rampant shortages. The Ministry of Food enforced a rationing system, which inevitably led to black markets that flourished even after the war ended. People traded with neighbours, and each village became a bartering network. This shadowy system serves as backdrop for this classic Miss Marple mystery. Neighbours slip into and from one another's homes, illegally trading goods: a pound of sugar for a pound of bacon, an extra yard of cloth for a pound of butter. Alibis become meaningless. This recipe isn't for the chocolate cake that Mitzi baked for Dora "Bunny" Bunner's birthday celebration, but Patrick Simmons probably would die for this delicious chocolate cake, too.

*continues*

## CAKE

1¾ cups (210 grams) bleached all-purpose (white) flour

2 cups (400 grams) granulated white sugar

¾ cup (90 grams) cocoa powder

1½ teaspoons baking soda

¾ teaspoon salt

½ cup (112 grams) unsalted butter, plus more for greasing

2 large eggs

1 cup (240 millilitres) buttermilk

1 tablespoon vanilla extract

1½ ounces (45 millilitres) espresso

## FROSTING

½ cup (112 grams) unsalted butter, softened

⅔ cup (80 grams) cocoa powder

1 teaspoon vanilla extract

1 cup (130 grams) confectioners' (powdered or icing) sugar

¼–½ cup (60–120 millilitres) whole milk

1. Preheat the oven to 350°F (180°C).

2. Lightly grease 2 round 9-inch (22-centimetre) cake pans.

3. In a large bowl, mix the flour, sugar, cocoa, baking soda, and salt.

4. In a medium bowl, melt the butter and beat the eggs, buttermilk, and vanilla extract into it.

5. Add the wet ingredients to the dry and mix until smooth.

6. Stir in the espresso and ½ cup (120 millilitres) hot water.

7. Divide the batter between the pans, bake for 30–35 minutes, and toothpick-test for doneness.

8. Let the cakes rest for 1–2 minutes, remove them from the pans, and let them cool to room temperature.

9. When the cakes have cooled, make the frosting. In a medium bowl, mix the butter, cocoa powder, vanilla extract, confectioners' sugar, and milk.

10. Spread the frosting evenly over the top of one cake, place the other cake on top, and spread the frosting evenly over the top and sides of the stacked cake.

# MIDDLE-EASTERN TURKEY STUFFING

"Yes, yes—and foie gras—Strasburg foie gras—and perhaps caviar—
and then we have a dish with fish—very nice—a fish from the Tigris,
but all with sauce and mushrooms. And then there is a turkey stuffed
in the way we have it at my home—with rice and raisins and spice—
and all cooked so! . . . We will have a long dinner that goes on for
hours. It will be very nice."

—MARCUS TIO, *They Came to Baghdad*, 1951

### ❧ SERVES 8 ❧

With its anti-communists, anti-capitalists, diplomats, and secret agents, this thriller reflects the changing politics in Britain and the rest of the world following World War II. In and around Baghdad, still regarded as the jewel of the Middle East, Christie gives us a Madame Defarge character, an archaeological dig, American bankers, government spies, and a new world order.

Situated on the banks of the Tigris, Baghdad has served as a cultural capital for most of its history as an integral part of the Sumerian, Assyrian, Babylonian, Persian, and Roman empires. It also functioned as a commercial and intellectual centre of the Muslim world, but the Mongol Empire destroyed it in the 1200s. In 1932, the kingdom gained full independence, and Baghdad regained its previous status as an international hub. In the novel, the jovial host of the Tio Hotel plans a delicious multi-cultural dinner that celebrates that status for protagonist Victoria Jones, and Christie describes the menu in mouth-watering detail. As with any turkey stuffing, European or Middle Eastern, this stuffing can go into a bird for roasting or serve as a side dish.

*continues*

2 shallots

2 medium cloves garlic

1 small (approximately 200 grams) sweet cooking apple

¼ cup (56 grams) salted butter

1½ cups (315 grams) long-grain white rice

½ cup (85 grams) golden raisins (sultanas)

2 cloves

6 peppercorns

¼ cinnamon stick

½ teaspoon allspice

½ teaspoon ground nutmeg

Salt

1 tablespoon finely chopped fresh mint (optional)

---

1. Finely chop the shallots and garlic and peel, core, and shred the apple.

2. In a medium pot over medium-low heat, melt the butter.

3. Add the shallots and cook until they become translucent, about 3–4 minutes, stirring often.

4. While the shallots are cooking, set a kettle filled with at least 3 cups (720 millilitres) of water over medium-high heat to boil.

5.   Add the rice to the shallots and stir well to coat the grains evenly in the butter.

6.   Add the garlic, apples, raisins, and all the spices except the salt. Stir well.

7.   Add 3 cups (720 millilitres) of boiling water and a generous pinch of salt.

8.   Cover, increase the heat to high, and bring to a boil.

9.   Reduce the heat to low and simmer gently, without lifting the lid, for 15 minutes.

10.  Remove from the heat and let it rest, without stirring, for 5 minutes.

11.  Fluff the rice, remove the cinnamon stick and cloves, and salt to taste.

12.  If making the recipe as a side dish, serve hot with fresh mint sprinkled on top. If using as stuffing, let it cool to room temperature before stuffing the bird.

# A PERFECT
# OMELETTE

"I have given Mrs. Summerhayes a cookery book and have also taught her personally how to make an omelette. *Bon Dieu*, what I suffered in that house!"

—HERCULE POIROT, *Mrs. McGinty's Dead*, 1952

### ⚜ SERVES 1 ⚜

Omelettes have played a role in every food culture in the world. Ancient Romans, Persians, Japanese, and Aztecs all discovered that eggs and heat, paired with almost any other ingredient, make a great meal. An innkeeper served an omelette to Napoléon Bonaparte that so impressed him that he ordered all the eggs in town be used to create a huge omelette for his army the next day. The French town of Bessières, near Toulouse, commemorates this event with an annual omelette festival. In Spain, food legend has it that, during the First Carlist War, a civil war in the 1830s, General Tomás de Zumalacárregui e Imaz whipped together eggs, potatoes, and onions as a cheap and easy way to feed his soldiers besieging Bilbao, thereby creating the renowned tortilla Española. When the cheerfully disheveled Ariadne Oliver and the punctiliously refined Hercule Poirot first encounter each other in this mystery, she has tossed an apple core from the window of her car, which hits him on the cheek. Unfortunately for the Belgian detective, he must leave his urban comforts to investigate this case, staying in a country guesthouse where he endures undercooked fare. In the end, having taught Maureen Summerhayes how to make a perfect omelette every time, he and his hosts part on good terms. Seven years later, in *Cat among the Pigeons*, Poirot will hear from a young schoolgirl that her Aunt Maureen makes smashing omelettes. He replies that he hasn't lived in vain.

2 tablespoons salted butter

2 large eggs

2 tablespoons whole milk

Salt and pepper

Mushrooms, grated Cheddar
   cheese, fine herbs, or seafood for
   filling (optional)

1. In a medium frying pan over medium heat, melt the butter.

2. Into a small bowl, crack the eggs and beat well.

3. Add the milk to the eggs and salt and pepper to taste. Mix well.

4. When the pan becomes hot enough to make a drop of water hiss, pour in the egg mixture. Do not stir. Cook for 1 minute, cover, and cook for 3 more minutes.

5. When the center has set firmly, turn the omelette over and cook for 1 more minute.

6. Add filling of choice down the center of the eggs, then gently fold half the omelette over, lining up the edges.

7. Cook for 1 more minute until the filling warms.

8. Slide the omelette onto a plate and serve.

# WEEKEND SALISBURY STEAK

"The meal was not a particularly appetising one. It was indifferently cooked and indifferently served."

—from *They Do It with Mirrors*, 1952

### ❧ SERVES 4 ❧

As a young woman, Miss Marple studied at a finishing school in Italy with other young women from wealthier backgrounds. From time to time, her friends from those years invite her to London for a meal or perhaps to the theater. In this novel, American socialite Ruth van Rydock, one such friend, has summoned her to London because Ruth is worried about her sister, Caroline Serrocold, also a friend to Miss Marple. Mrs. Serrocold owns Stonygates, a large Victorian country estate that hosts a school for delinquent boys. In the spirit of rehabilitating the lads, one or two of them dine with the Serrocolds each night, replicating a traditional family atmosphere. The school serves plain, nutritional meals made according to the government's postwar rationing rules. Many institutional English dishes rest on a foundation of ground beef and brown sauce, usually cooked apathetically. Meals served in the Great Hall at Stonygates likely included hotpot, shepherd's pie, toad in the hole, and Salisbury steak. At home, when writer Raymond West, her nephew, visits of a weekend, Miss Marple would make a much more tasty version of that last dish, perhaps like this.

1 medium yellow onion

5 ounces (140 grams) mushrooms

1 large egg

⅓ cup (50 grams) breadcrumbs

1 pound (454 grams) medium to lean ground (mince) beef

2 tablespoons ketchup

2½ teaspoons Worcestershire sauce

2 teaspoons mustard powder

1 tablespoon olive oil

2 tablespoons salted butter

3 tablespoons all-purpose (white) flour

2 cups (470 millilitres) beef broth

2 teaspoons mustard

Salt and pepper

1. Halve the onion; grate 1 half and finely chop the other. Slice the mushrooms and in a small bowl beat the egg.

2. In a large bowl, mix the breadcrumbs with the grated onion, then, one at a time, add the beef, beaten egg, ketchup, ½ teaspoon of Worcestershire sauce, and the mustard powder. Mix until fully combined after adding each ingredient.

3. Divide the beef mixture into 6 equal parts, making 1 patty with each.

4. In a frying pan over high heat, add the olive oil and cook each patty for 1 minute, or until browned, on each side. Remove and set aside.

5. Reduce the heat to medium. Add the chopped onions to the pan and cook until the onions become translucent, about 5–6 minutes.

6. Add the sliced mushrooms and cook for 2–3 more minutes.

7. Reduce the heat to medium-low and add the butter. When the butter has melted, add the flour and cook for 30 seconds, stirring constantly.

8. While continuing to stir constantly, slowly add the broth, mustard, the remaining 2 teaspoons of Worcestershire sauce, and salt and pepper to taste.

9. Put the patties back in the pan along with any juices collected on the plate. Cook for 5–7 minutes. If the gravy thickens too quickly, add a little water but no more than 1 cup (240 millilitres).

10. Plate the steaks and top them with the gravy.

# WHOLE CHICKEN SOUP

"Cold lunch, of course, it had to be. Ham and chicken and tongue
and salad. With cold lemon soufflé and apple tart to follow. Hot soup
first—and he'd better go along and see that Marjorie had got it on
ready to serve, for they'd be back in a minute or two now for certain."

—LANSCOMBE, *After the Funeral*, 1953

### ⸙ SERVES 10 ⸙

In this dark mystery, Christie explores the postwar collapse of an extended
family whose members continue following prewar traditions and customs as if
nothing had changed. Richard Abernethie, master of Enderby Hall, has died,
and his family has gathered at his home for the reading of the will. Mortimer,
Richard's only son, died during the war, which leaves matters to Timothy,
Richard's only surviving brother; Helen, widow of Richard's brother Leo;
Cora Lansquenet, his surviving but estranged sister; and the three grown
children of his predeceased brothers and sisters. In the upper classes, after a
funeral and before the reading of a will, the family traditionally has a luncheon.
Servants, including Marjorie, the cook, attend the funeral service but not the
burial, returning to the house to prepare the lunch. The spirits at Enderby Hall
lift considerably after a delicious meal featuring Marjorie's excellent chicken
soup and plenty of customary cold dishes, all accompanied by several bottles
of excellent Chablis.

2¼ pounds (1 kilogram) whole chicken

3 leeks

2 stalks celery

2 shallots

1½ tablespoons olive oil

⅓ cup (80 millilitres) dry white wine

2 sprigs thyme, plus more for garnish

2 bay leaves

1¼ cups (300 millilitres) heavy (double) cream

⅓ cup (40 grams) bleached all-purpose (white) flour

Salt

1. Skin the chicken and cut it into pieces. Coarsely chop the leeks and celery. Cut the shallots into wedges.

2. In a large pot over medium heat, add the olive oil. When the oil is hot, add the chicken and fry, uncovered, for about 10 minutes, turning regularly.

3. While the chicken is frying, set a kettle filled with at least 8½ cups (2 litres) of water over medium-high heat to boil.

4. Once the chicken has browned lightly, add the wine, leeks, celery, shallots, 2 sprigs of thyme, and the bay leaves.

5. Add 8½ cups (2 litres) of boiling water. Reduce the heat to medium-low. Cover the pot and simmer for 45 minutes, until the vegetables and chicken become tender.

6. Remove from the heat, remove the thyme and bay leaves, and let the soup cool for 30 minutes.

7. Remove the chicken from the pot. Separate the meat from the bones, reserving the meat and discarding the bones, fat, and gristle.

*continues*

8.  Chop the chicken meat into small pieces. Reserve 1 cup (140 grams) of the chicken and return the rest to the pan.

9.  Using a hand mixer or immersion blender, process everything in the pot until smooth. Alternatively, you can mash it by hand or transfer everything to a food processor or blender and blend.

10. In a medium bowl, add the cream and whisk the flour into it.

11. Stir a few tablespoons of the soup into the cream mixture, then pour all the cream mixture into the pot, stirring constantly over medium-low heat until it thickens, about 8–10 minutes.

12. Season with salt to taste and stir the remaining chicken into the soup.

13. Divide the soup into bowls and garnish each with half a sprig of thyme.

# SIXPENCE BLACKBIRD PIE

"'You can't tell me anything about blackbirds, can you?'
She stared at him.
'Blackbirds? Blackbirds? You mean the ones in the pie?'
They *would* be in the pie, the Inspector thought to himself.
He merely said, 'When was this?'
'Oh! Three or four months ago—and there were some on
Father's desk, too. He was furious.'"

—INSPECTOR NEELE AND ELAINE FORTESCUE,
*A Pocket Full of Rye*, 1953

### ❧ YIELDS 1 PIE ❧

Christie delighted in the macabre side of nursery rhymes and used several as titles
for her mysteries. In this one, Rex Fortescue, patriarch of Yewtree Lodge, dies
at his office in the city; his trophy wife dies in the parlor after having tea; and the
maid is found dead with a clothespin on her nose. When Miss Marple arrives
to investigate the death of her former maid, she notes the similarity of events to
"Sing a Song of Sixpence." Several months earlier, someone had delivered a real
blackbird pie to the house. Food writer and TV host Steven Raichlen describes the
original medieval dish as "an enormous pie crust that had a wooden scaffolding
inside, so it was in effect baked hollow. Then you cut a trapdoor in the bottom, you
put live birds in the pie, cracked open the top, and the birds would come fluttering
out through the dining room." The British ate blackbirds well into the Victorian
era; Harriet de Salis included this recipe in *Dressed Game and Poultry à la Mode*,
published in 1888. Substitute small Cornish game hens for the blackbirds.

*continues*

## PIE

½ cup (120 millilitres) whole milk

6 stale rolls

1½ ounces (42 grams) salted butter

1 shallot, chopped

2 tablespoons fresh chopped parsley

¼ teaspoon ground nutmeg

Salt and pepper

2 small egg yolks

6 blackbirds, plucked and cleaned, or 6 small Cornish game hens

½ pound (225 grams) ground (mince) beef

4 small egg yolks, hard boiled

Puff pastry to cover 1 pie

## SAUCE

1 small yellow onion

2 tablespoons salted butter

4 tablespoons (32 grams) all-purpose (white) flour

1 cup (470 millilitres) beef stock

Salt and pepper

---

1. Preheat the oven to 325°F (165°C).

2. In a saucepan over medium heat, add the milk, rolls, butter, shallot, and parsley. Season with the nutmeg and salt and pepper to taste. Add the 2 egg yolks and stir until it forms a thick paste.

3. Stuff the mixture into the birds.

4. Next make the sauce. Finely chop the onion.

5. In a small frying pan over medium heat, add the butter and onions and fry until brown, approximately 5–6 minutes.

6. Slowly stir in the flour, stirring constantly.

7. Gradually add the stock and season with salt and pepper to taste.

8. Cook, stirring constantly, until the sauce thickens, about 15 minutes. Remove from the heat.

9. In a medium frying pan over medium heat, fry the beef until it is cooked through and crumbly, about 5–6 minutes.

10. Line the bottom of a large pie dish with the cooked beef.

11. Lay the 6 birds in the dish. Crumble the cooked egg yolks among them.

12. Pour the brown sauce over the birds, cover with puff pastry, and bake for 1 hour 15 minutes.

13. Serve hot.

# MOROCCAN MINT TEA

"In due course glasses of mint tea were brought. To Hilary who did not
like sugar with her tea, it was somewhat of an ordeal to drink it."

—from *Destination Unknown*, 1954

### ❦ YIELDS 1 POT ❧

Christie wrote *Destination Unknown* just after the real-life case of Bruno Pon-
tecorvo, an Italian nuclear physicist who defected from Britain to the Soviet
Union in 1950. In this novel, a scientist has disappeared, which concerns the
government. They recruit a despondent Hilary Craven to help, and her mission begins in Morocco, where she wanders the market stalls and soaks in the
sights, sounds, and tastes of Fez, Casablanca, and Marrakesh. Moroccan mint
tea consists of green tea prepared with spearmint and sugar, a beverage that
depends on international trade for importing tea and sugar to mix with local
mint. Moroccans drink this tea throughout the day as a social activity. Tea bars
in North Africa function as analogs to the pubs of Britain.

**2 tablespoons loose green tea**　　　　**1 large bunch fresh spearmint**
**3–4 tablespoons granulated white**
**sugar**

1. Set a kettle filled with 5 cups (1.25 litres) of filtered water over
   medium-high heat until it almost boils but not quite.

2. Pour 1 cup (240 millilitres) of hot water into a teapot and return the
   kettle to the heat until it boils.

3. Swirl the hot water in the teapot, drain, and discard the water.

4. Add the tea to the teapot.

5.  Add the remaining 4 cups (1 litre) boiling water to the teapot and steep, covered with a cozy, for 2 minutes.

6.  Stir in the sugar and mint and steep for 3–4 more minutes.

7.  Strain the loose tea and serve in small traditional glasses or teacups.

# SOUTHERN ITALIAN SPAGHETTI AND MEATBALLS

"Poirot sat down . . . and busied himself with keeping his moustaches out of the excellent minestrone which was served by a small active Italian manservant from a big tureen. This was followed by a piping hot dish of spaghetti and meatballs."

—from *Hickory Dickory Dock*, 1955

## ❧ SERVES 4 ❧

In the mid-1950s, students from around the world came to London to study and work, bringing their different cultures and ideals with them. Mrs. Hubbard—the widowed sister of Felicity Lemon, Poirot's secretary—runs a student hostel. Maria, the hostel's Italian cook, has lived in England for years but seems much less acclimatized to English culture than the newly arrived students. She criticizes English food in general and especially English stew, which horrifies her with a drama befitting a chef. The evening that Poirot comes, she forgoes the reviled English stew and treats the detective to her best efforts. In Italy, pasta dishes cooked with meat date as far back as the Middle Ages. But spaghetti and meatballs originated not in Italy but rather among Italian immigrant communities in America, where meat proved much less expensive and featured in daily cooking more often than in the old country. In modern Italy, certain dishes approximate spaghetti with meatballs, though only in certain regions and towns. In Southern Italy, the dish has smaller meatballs that characteristically combine beef and pork and cook in the spaghetti sauce, as in this recipe.

## MEATBALLS

½ pound (225 grams) lean ground (mince) beef

½ pound (225 grams) lean ground (mince) pork

1 cup (150 grams) fresh breadcrumbs

1 tablespoon freshly grated Parmesan cheese, plus more for serving

¼ teaspoon ground black pepper

1 clove garlic, finely chopped

1 large egg, beaten

## SAUCE

¼ cup (60 millilitres) olive oil

1 medium yellow onion, chopped

5 cloves garlic, finely chopped

Two 28-ounce cans (785 grams) whole peeled tomatoes

2 teaspoons salt

½ teaspoon red pepper flakes

1 bay leaf

One 6-ounce can (168 grams) tomato paste

1 tablespoon fresh chopped basil

½ pound dry spaghetti

Salt

---

1. First make the meatballs. In a large bowl, combine the beef, pork, breadcrumbs, cheese, pepper, garlic, and egg. Mix well.

2. Form the meat mixture into 12–16 small balls, return them to the large bowl, cover it with plastic, and refrigerate.

3. Next make the sauce. In a large saucepan over medium-low heat, add the olive oil, onion, and garlic and sauté, stirring regularly, until the onion becomes translucent, about 5–6 minutes.

4. Stir in the peeled tomatoes, salt, red pepper flakes, and bay leaf. Cover, reduce the heat to low, and simmer for 1 hour 30 minutes.

5. Stir in the tomato paste and basil, then add the refrigerated meatballs. Simmer for 30 more minutes. When done, remove the bay leaf and discard.

6. While the sauce is simmering, make the pasta. Fill a large pot half-

*continues*

way full of water. Add 1 tablespoon (17 grams) of salt per pound (450 grams) of dry pasta.

7. Cover the pot and set over medium-high heat to boil.

8. When the water boils, add the noodles and cook according to the package directions.

9. Drain the spaghetti, add the sauce and meatballs, and mix well.

10. Serve on a large platter with freshly grated Parmesan on the side and pair with a robust Italian red wine, such as Chianti.

# A FULL ENGLISH AT NASSE HOUSE

"Poirot came down to breakfast on the following morning at nine-thirty. A row of hot dishes on an electric heater. Sir George was eating a full-sized Englishman's breakfast of scrambled eggs, bacon and kidneys."

—from *Dead Man's Folly*, 1956

### ❦ SERVES 2 ❦

This novel reunites Poirot and Mrs. Oliver at a fête held at Nasse House, a country estate similar to Greenway. Christie modeled many of the locations in this mystery on her own home: the tennis court, the lawns where the fête takes place, the ferry landing where the old man is found dead, and the boathouse where the murder hunt ends. In this novel, food separates the traditional Englishman from the rest of the guests and plays an important role in the murder. Who took tea to the body in the boathouse? As a full meal, an English breakfast traditionally includes back bacon, eggs, grilled tomatoes, mushrooms, fried bread or toast, sausages, and baked beans. Regional variations feature kippers, black pudding, fried onions, deviled kidneys, or oatcakes.

*continues*

4 sausages

4 slices bacon

4 slices ham

One 14-ounce can (392 grams)
baked beans

4 mushrooms, stalks trimmed

Salt and pepper

Olive oil or butter for coating

1 tomato, thickly sliced

4 slices day-old bread

4 eggs

---

1.  Preheat the oven to 170°F (80°C) or its lowest setting and prepare breakfast in the following order.

2.  First cook the meat. In a large cast-iron skillet over low heat, cook the sausages for 10 minutes, turning regularly.

3.  Increase the heat to medium, add the bacon, and cook to preference.

4.  Transfer the sausages and bacon to an oven-safe dish, add the ham, cover with aluminum foil, and place in the oven.

5.  Next make the beans, mushrooms, and tomatoes. Into a small pot over low heat, add the can of beans.

6.  While the beans are warming, season the mushrooms with salt and pepper to taste and lightly coat them with oil or butter.

7.  Place the whole mushrooms, stalk side up, in the cast-iron skillet. Cook over medium heat for 1–2 minutes, turn over, and cook for 2–3 more minutes.

8.  Brush the tomato slices with oil, season with salt and pepper to taste, and place them in the cast-iron skillet with the mushrooms over medium-low heat for 2 minutes. Don't move the tomato slices while they cook.

9.  Gently flip the tomato slices and fry for 2 more minutes.

10. Transfer the tomatoes and mushrooms from the skillet to an oven-safe plate and place it in the oven with the meat.

11. Next make the fried bread. In a medium cast-iron skillet over medium heat, add a little oil or butter. When hot, place as many slices of bread as will fit in the pan and cook for 2–3 minutes per side, until golden brown.

12. Remove the fried bread, wrap it with aluminum foil, and keep warm in the oven. Place 2 oven-safe serving plates in the oven as well.

13. Lastly make the eggs. For scrambled, in a medium bowl, whisk together the eggs and 1 teaspoon of water.

14. In a frying pan over low heat, pour in the eggs and stir constantly as they cook. Remove the eggs from the heat when they have set but still look moist, about 2 minutes. Season with salt and pepper to taste.

15. For fried, crack the eggs straight into the frying pan. Cook to preference, flipping if desired. Season with salt and pepper to taste.

16. Remove all food from the oven, plate on the warmed serving plates with the eggs, and serve immediately.

# LUCY EYELESBARROW'S MUSHROOM SOUP

"'Mushroom soup—out of a tin, I suppose?'
'Certainly not. I made it. . . . Half a pound of mushrooms,
chicken stock, milk, a roux of butter and flour, and lemon juice.'"

—DR. QUIMPER AND LUCY EYELESBARROW,
*4.50 from Paddington*, 1957

### ⚜ SERVES 2 ⚜

By the late 1950s, Christie is writing Miss Marple as aging but active. After Christmas shopping in London, her good friend Elspeth McGillicuddy comes to St. Mary Mead and en route sees a man strangling a woman in a fur coat on a passing train. Officials find no body, however, and dismiss Mrs. McGillicuddy's report. Undaunted, she tells her story to Miss Marple, who determines that the body must have been pushed off the train onto the grounds of Rutherford Hall. Miss Marple wastes no time recruiting Lucy Eyelesbarrow and getting her "hired" there for the holiday season. By this time, the servant classes had dwindled in number, and Lucy fills a profitable niche. Wealthy people will pay handsomely for domestic peace, so she handles fussy children, cantankerous old men, sick relatives, and even dogs. She makes beds, has "no airs about her," and, best of all, she cooks brilliantly.

3 tablespoons salted butter

½ pound (225 grams) mushrooms, sliced

Salt and pepper

Lemon juice

1 cup (250 millilitres) chicken broth

1 tablespoon bleached all-purpose (white) flour

1 cup (250 millilitres) whole milk

Lemon zest for garnish

1. In a medium pan over medium-low heat, add 2 tablespoons butter, the mushrooms, salt, pepper, and lemon juice to taste. Sauté for 4–5 minutes.

2. Add the chicken broth, stir, and simmer over medium-low heat for 10 minutes.

3. Meanwhile, make the roux. In a small pan over low heat, melt 1 tablespoon butter.

4. Add the flour, then whisk in the milk. When it begins to thicken, remove from the heat.

5. Add the roux to the soup and stir well. Cook for 10 more minutes, stirring regularly until it thickens.

6. Divide the soup between soup bowls and garnish with lemon zest.

# WILD BLACKBERRY PIE

"Why, those kids even had their vegetables sieved, up to nearly five years old, and their milk sterilised and the water tested and their calories weighed and their vitamins computed! . . . I told her to let 'em eat a few blackberries from the hedges."

—DR. MACMASTER, *Ordeal by Innocence*, 1958

### ❧ YIELDS ONE 9-INCH (22-CENTIMETRE) PIE ❧

In one of Christie's darkest novels, memories of a murder haunt a family, especially when a new witness stirs up the past and makes them question their memories. Christie also uses the children's memories of food to contrast their lives before and during the war. Michael, one of the adopted children, has colorful, exciting memories of his mother and especially the fish and chips of London, whereas his memories of Sunny Point with his wealthy adoptive family run boring and bland. Dr. MacMaster would have prescribed a pie made from berries that the children had picked themselves.

4 cups (600 grams) fresh blackberries

¾ cup (150 grams) granulated white sugar

½ cup (60 grams) all-purpose (white) flour

One 9-inch (22-centimetre) double-crust pie pastry, frozen or freshly made

1 tablespoon whole milk

1. Preheat the oven to 425°F (220°C).

2. In a large bowl, mix 3½ cups (525 grams) of the berries with ½ cup (100 grams) of the sugar and all the flour.

3. Place 1 layer of the pie crust into a 9-inch (22-centimetre) pie pan.

4. Spoon the berry mixture into the pie crust and add the last ½ cup (75 grams) of berries on top.

5. Cut the remaining pastry in strips and lay them across the top of the pie in a lattice pattern. Seal the pie by pinching the edges of the 2 pastry layers together all the way around.

6. Brush the pastry lattice with the milk and sprinkle the remaining sugar over it.

7. Bake for 15 minutes.

8. Reduce the heat to 375°F (190°C) and bake for 20–25 more minutes, until the crust turns golden brown.

9. Remove from the oven and let the pie cool to room temperature.

# MEADOWBANK MARVEL

"The food here is jolly good. Yesterday we had chicken for lunch, and we had lovely homemade cakes for tea."

—JENNIFER SUTCLIFFE, *Cat among the Pigeons*, 1959

## ⅊ SERVES 4 ⅊

The Public Schools Act of 1868 reformed seven of England's leading "public" boarding schools for boys, including Eton, Harrow, and Rugby, many of which had begun centuries earlier as charity schools founded by religious orders. Each school now had a board of governors overseeing a broad-based curriculum instead of the clergy-taught, classics-only approach of the past. Students paid fees, and scholarship programs admitted meritorious students from less privileged backgrounds. Girls' boarding schools arose more recently than those ancient institutions for boys, but they largely followed the same outline, as does Christie's Meadowbank School for Girls, which has it all: a respected founder, expensive fees, royalty, a broad curriculum, a cricket team, jewels, a foreign coup, government spies, and a tennis racket. In this plot, food doesn't receive much attention, but Meadowbank's cooks no doubt echoed the dishes served at sibling schools, such as Eton mess, traditionally proffered at the college's annual cricket match against Harrow. Some claim that the mess of crushed fruit honours a serving accident, others that the smashing was intentional. Either way, Meadowbank doesn't approve of smashing, whether accidental or purposeful, so this dessert is very well behaved indeed.

**4 large ripe peaches**

**1 cup (240 millilitres) heavy (double) cream**

**12 Literary Luncheon Meringues (page 155)**

---

1.  Peel the peaches, remove the pits, and slice the fruit into medium pieces. Preserve the juice from peeling and slicing and reserve 4 slices for garnish. Set aside.

2.  With a hand mixer or immersion blender, whip the cream in a small bowl until it forms soft peaks.

3.  Divide the meringues among the 4 serving bowls.

4.  Spoon the peaches and juice over the meringues in each bowl.

5.  Top with whipped cream and garnish with a peach slice.

1960s

A S the deprivations of the postwar period faded into the past, the swinging 1960s brought economic prosperity and cultural popularity to Britain. Industry recovered, shops thrived, and life became more colourful and flavourful. Britons bought dishwashers, went on holidays around the world, and listened to the Beatles, the Kinks, and the Rolling Stones. Immigration and youth culture—which transformed over the decade into counterculture—combined to change eating habits in Britain as well. As a way of life, the young eagerly embraced American hamburgers and milkshakes, Indian curries, and Chinese takeout.

Christie, now in her 70s, approached the decade with some trepidation. Mixing Americans, foreign settings, and modern ideas, she often combined crimes from the past with uncertain futures. *The Pale Horse*, her first published novel of the decade, begins with the protagonist munching a sandwich made famous by American rock star Elvis Presley. Unimpressed with the new decade, Poirot has grown older and fustier. In *The Clocks*, he barely leaves his armchair while rereading golden age mysteries. In *Third Girl*, a young girl tells him flat out that he's too old. As London modernizes around him, Poirot remains resolutely unwilling to embrace change. Tommy and Tuppence Beresford are growing older, too, but with more grace. Their respective red and black hair has become peppered with gray, and they have retired in *By the Pricking of My Thumbs*. In 1968, the year that novel appeared, Christie's husband, Max Mallowan, received a knighthood for his achievements in archaeology, which granted Christie the style of Lady Mallowan.

Miss Marple, the oldest of Christie's sleuths, ironically leads the charge into the future. In *The Mirror Crack'd from Side to Side*—which takes its name from Alfred Tennyson's "The Lady of Shalott," written in the early Victorian era—American movie stars come to St. Mary Mead. The contrasts among the villagers, people living in a new subdivision, and the movie people offer a case study of how village life continues to change. St. Mary Mead even has a supermarket now. In *A Caribbean Mystery*, Miss Marple holidays on the fictitious island of St. Honoré, where she encounters new foods, including passion fruit for breakfast, which she quite likes. On holiday again in *At Bertram's Hotel*, she enjoys the Edwardian nostalgia, but it doesn't feel right. Times have changed, and everyone must change with them.

# CHELSEA BANANA AND BACON SANDWICH

"It seemed an odd juxtaposition to me. Bananas I connected with my childhood—or occasionally flambé with sugar and rum. Bacon, in my mind, was firmly associated with eggs. However, when in Chelsea, eat as Chelsea does. I agreed to a nice banana and bacon sandwich."

—MARK EASTERBROOK, *The Pale Horse,* 1961

## ❧ YIELDS 1 SANDWICH ❧

The title of this novel comes from the name of a small country village inn, itself inspired by the Bible's Book of Revelation. In that text, God holds a book secured with seven seals. The Lion of Judah or the Lamb of God opens four seals, which call forth Conquest on a white horse, War on a red one, Famine on black, and Death astride a pale horse. A dying woman's last confession leads the narrator, Mark Easterbrook, and Ariadne Oliver to the inn, where three self-proclaimed witches live. But before leaping headlong into this riot of ancient allusions to the apocalypse and the supernatural, the story begins in Chelsea, the beating heart of Swinging London. Elvis Presley, who ruled the airwaves of the early 1960s, made this cutting-edge, sweet-and-savoury sandwich, which originated in America, internationally famous.

*continues*

3 slices bacon

1 ripe banana

2 tablespoons unsalted butter

2 slices bread of choice

½ tablespoon maple syrup (optional)

---

1. In a large cast-iron pan over medium heat, cook the bacon to preference. Remove from the pan, set on a plate lined with paper towels to drain, and drain the grease from the pan.

2. In a small bowl, mash the banana. Set aside.

3. Butter 1 slice of bread and place it, butter side down, on another plate.

4. Spread half the mashed banana on the unbuttered side and top with all the cooked bacon.

5. Butter the second slice of bread and place it, buttered side up, atop the bacon.

6. Using a spatula, transfer the sandwich to the pan and grill both sides over medium heat until they turn golden brown, about 3–4 minutes per side.

7. Drizzle with maple syrup if desired and serve hot.

# HOLLYWOOD DAIQUIRI

"Hemlock in the cocktails, wasn't it? Something of that kind."

—JOHNNY JETHROE, *The Mirror Crack'd from Side to Side*, 1962

### ⁂ MAKES 1 COCKTAIL ⁂

In 1930, St. Mary Mead has a manor house, six large homes, small cottages, a rooming home, a church and vicarage, train station, inn, and several small shops, including a butcher and grocer. In 1942, Colonel and Mrs. Bantry live in the manor house; the village has a new post office, a fishmonger on the High Street, and its own policeman; and a young man connected to the film industry has rented a cottage near town. Two decades later, the village has changed further. It now features a supermarket, taxi service, and a new housing development. After Colonel Bantry's death, Mrs. Bantry has sold the manor house to Marina Gregg, an American movie star, and her director husband, moving quite happily into the gardener's cottage on the estate. Gregg brings glamour and fame to the village, but death never lingers far behind. After drinking a Daiquiri at a party hosted by the movie star, a local woman dies. Christie loves a killer cocktail. In the 18th century, British sailors drank lots of rum. Cutting it with water and lime juice curbed rampant inebriation at sea, helped prevent scurvy, and created Old Grog, one of the first rum cocktails (named for Admiral Edward Vernon, known for the grogram coat he wore). By the end of the 19th century, Facundo Bacardí y Massó had pioneered a new, lighter, drier style of Cuban rum, and, several decades later, Prohibition pushed American cocktail culture offshore into the Caribbean, creating conditions perfect for this cocktail. It takes its name from a village on the island's southern coast, named by Cuba's native Taíno people.

*continues*

**1½ ounces (45 millilitres) light rum**
**¾ ounce (20 millilitres) lime juice**

**½ ounce (15 millilitres) Simple Syrup (page 55)**
**Lime slice, for garnish**

---

1. Into a cocktail shaker filled with ice, pour the rum, lime juice, and simple syrup.

2. Shake well for 30 seconds and strain into a chilled cocktail glass.

3. Garnish with a lime slice—not hemlock.

# FRENCH ROLLS

" 'I've started on Crescents. Houses in crescents is what I mean.'

'I didn't suppose you meant bakers' shops with French rolls in them, though, come to think of it, there's no reason why not. Some of them places make an absolute fetish of producing French croissants that aren't really French. Keep 'em in a deep freeze nowadays like everything else. That's why nothing tastes of anything nowadays.' "

—COLIN LAMB AND COLONEL BECK, *The Clocks*, 1963

### ❧ YIELDS 18 CROISSANTS ☙

Christie wrote few spy thrillers. Her own thrillers focused on murder, of course, but not the ethical and geopolitical issues that overran spy stories of the period, such as Ian Fleming's James Bond novels. As in Alfred Hitchcock's *Rear Window*, released a decade earlier, this mystery features a witness with a broken leg who sits all day, watching the neighbours, and provides the essential clue to solving a murder. MI5 agent Colin Lamb, meanwhile, searches everywhere for the answer to a clue found in a dead spy's pocket: a sketch of a crescent moon beside the letter M and the number 61. Christie loves a double entendre, and the exchange between Lamb and Beck plays on the double meaning of "crescents." The colonel's housekeeper would have spent years refining her recipe to please her employer. If you don't want to spend years perfecting this one, there's no shame in buying croissants from a good local French bakery.

2 teaspoons (8 grams) active dry yeast

2 cups (240 grams) all-purpose (white) flour, plus more for dusting

¼ cup (50 grams) fine sugar

½ tablespoon salt

⅝ cup (140 grams) unsalted butter

½ cup (120 millilitres) whole milk, warm

1 large egg

*continues*

1. In a small glass, mix the yeast with ¼ cup (60 millilitres) warm water. Set aside to activate.

2. Into a large bowl, sift the flour, then stir in the sugar and salt.

3. Chop the butter into small pieces and coat them in the flour mixture.

4. Stir in the milk and activated yeast, then mix until the dough becomes stiff.

5. Wrap the dough in plastic and refrigerate for 1 hour.

6. On a floured surface, roll out the dough into a rectangle.

7. Fold the dough over into thirds, like a letter going into an envelope. Turn and roll out again into a rectangle. Repeat several times.

8. Roll the dough into a ball and wrap with plastic. Chill for 1 more hour.

9. Divide the dough in half and on a floured surface roll each half into a circle about ⅛ inch (3 millimetres) thick.

10. Cut the dough circles into wedges shaped like slices of pie. Starting at the wide end, roll each wedge up.

11. Line a baking sheet with parchment paper, place the unbaked croissants on it, and set the baking sheet in a warm area, such as near a sunny window. Cover loosely with a towel and let the dough rise until it doubles in size, about 2 hours.

12. Preheat the oven to 375°F (190°C).

13. Beat the egg, then lightly brush the risen dough with egg wash.

14. Bake for 20 minutes, until golden brown, and serve warm.

# GRILLED STEAK AT THE GOLDEN PALM

"But it was a steak knife, Mr. Daventry. Steaks were on the menu
that evening. Steak knives are kept sharp."

—INSPECTOR WESTON, *A Caribbean Mystery*, 1964

### ❧ SERVES 4 ❧

Miss Marple's nephew, novelist Raymond West, has paid for her to recover
from a recent illness at the Golden Palm Hotel on St. Honoré, a fictional
island in the Caribbean, and Christie uses the occasion to poke fun at preju-
dices about the elderly—or is it the English?—on holiday. The hotelier presses
Miss Marple to order English food instead of, for her, more exotic Caribbean
fare. Miss Marple assures him that new foods are one of the pleasures of going
abroad. Unconvinced, he continues pressing her with offers of bread and butter pudding. She refuses and digs into her passion fruit sundae "with cheerful
appreciation." Never underestimate Miss Marple or the crucial role of cutlery
in a murder mystery. This grilled steak, full of Caribbean flavour, recreates the
one that pleased Miss Marple on her trip to the Caribbean. Full of tomatoes,
peppers, and island spices, it will have you dreaming of a Caribbean holiday.

*continues*

1 shallot, finely chopped

1 cup (200 grams) chopped fresh tomatoes

½ Scotch bonnet pepper, finely chopped

2 tablespoons finely chopped fresh cilantro

2 tablespoons finely chopped fresh parsley

1 tablespoon finely chopped fresh thyme

¼ cup (60 millilitres) olive oil

1 pinch sea salt, plus more for seasoning

½ teaspoon freshly ground black pepper, plus more for seasoning

Juice of 1 lemon

Juice of 1 orange

Two 8-ounce (225-gram) top sirloin steaks

---

1. In a large bowl, mix together the shallot, tomatoes, Scotch bonnet pepper, and herbs. Wear gloves when handling the pepper.

2. Stir in the olive oil, salt, pepper, and citrus juices.

3. Rinse the steaks, pat them dry with paper towels, and set them in a large casserole dish. Pour half the marinade over the steaks, coating them evenly. Reserve the remaining marinade.

4. Marinate the steaks at room temperature for at least 1 hour.

5. Heat the grill to high. Place the steaks on the grill and cook them, 3 minutes per side for medium rare.

6. Transfer the steaks to a cutting board, tent them loosely with aluminum foil, and let them rest for 5 minutes.

7. Slice the steaks across the grain and drizzle with the reserved marinade.

8. Season with sea salt and freshly ground black pepper to taste and pair with a bottle of Malbec.

# OLD ENGLISH SEED CAKE

"'Seed cake? I haven't eaten seed cake for years. It is real seed cake?'
'Oh yes, my lady. The cook has had the recipe for years.
You'll enjoy it, I'm sure.'"

—SELINA HAZY AND HENRY, *At Bertram's Hotel*, 1965

### ❧ YIELDS 1 BUNDT CAKE ❧
### OR
### ❧ TWO 8-BY-4-INCH (20-BY-10-CENTIMETRE) LOAVES ❧

In this novel, Miss Marple enjoys another two-week holiday courtesy of her novelist nephew, this time in London. Bertram's Hotel, where she stays, conjures a bygone era with staff dressed as Edwardian servants. Impoverished aristocrats, including Lady Selina Hazy, receive special rates to further the illusion, and they dine on glorious Edwardian food for breakfast (a full English), lunch (beefsteak pudding), and tea (cakes served at 4 PM in the lobby). This display creates a convincing impression of an undiminished past and, likely a more important goal, attracts American tourists. Seed cake has a long and distinguished popularity in England. Hannah Glasse included three recipes for it in *The Art of Cookery Made Plain and Easy* (1747). In *Jane Eyre*, published a century later, Miss Temple shares one with Jane as an act of kindness in the dismal Lowood School. *Mrs. Beeton's Book of Household Management* (1861) features a recipe for the dish, and in *The Hobbit* (1937), Bilbo Baggins fetches seed cakes from his larder to share with uninvited guests. When next feeding guests, invited or otherwise, enjoy this traditional cake with A Perfect Cup of Tea (page 79).

*continues*

¾ cup (170 grams) unsalted butter, softened, plus more for greasing

2 cups (400 grams) granulated white sugar

4 medium eggs

4 teaspoons lemon peel, thinly sliced

3 cups (360 grams) all-purpose (white) flour

2½ teaspoons baking powder

½ teaspoon ground nutmeg

½ teaspoon ground cloves

1 cup (240 millilitres) whole milk

3 tablespoons caraway seeds

3 tablespoons anise seeds

3 tablespoons poppy seeds

1–2 tablespoons confectioners' (powdered or icing) sugar

---

1. Preheat the oven to 350°F (180°C).

2. With a stand mixer set to medium speed, cream the butter and sugar until fluffy.

3. Add the eggs, one at a time, then the lemon peel.

4. In a separate bowl, combine the flour, baking powder, nutmeg, and cloves.

5. Add ⅓ of the flour mixture to the egg mixture, then ⅓ cup of milk. Blend and repeat twice.

6. Grease a Bundt pan or 2 small loaf pans.

7. Pour ¼ of the batter into the pan(s) and sprinkle the batter with the caraway seeds.

8. Pour another ¼ of the batter into the pan(s) and sprinkle with the anise seeds.

9. Pour another ¼ of the batter into the pan(s) and sprinkle with the poppy seeds.

10. Pour the final ¼ of the batter into the pan(s) and bake for 1 hour.

11. Remove the cake(s) from the oven and cool on a rack for 10 minutes.

12. Remove the cake(s) from the pan(s) and cool on the rack for 10 more minutes.

13. Dust with the confectioners' sugar, cover, and allow to rest overnight.

# A PERFECT CUP OF HOT CHOCOLATE

"Poirot was sitting at the breakfast table. At his right
hand was a steaming cup of chocolate. . . . To accompany
the chocolate was a brioche."

—from *Third Girl*, 1966

## ⁕ SERVES 4 ⁕

Poirot begins this mystery with his favourite morning routine: eating a pastry
with a cup of hot chocolate. In the next scene, Poirot hears that he's too old
to help a potential client. Wounded, he calls his friend Ariadne Oliver, who
consoles him with more hot chocolate, of course. In the 1500s, the Spanish
brought cacao beans from Mexico to Europe, and hot chocolate became a
popular European beverage in the mid-1600s. Around 1828, Casparus van
Houten, a Dutchman, developed a hydraulic press to separate the cocoa butter
(what we call white chocolate) from the beans. The chocolaty remnants became
cocoa powder, which led to the development of bar chocolate and other tasty
morsels. Since 1894, Belgium has ranked as one of the world's foremost chocolate producers. No wonder Poirot enjoys it so much.

4 cups (1 litre) whole milk

1 vanilla pod

1 cinnamon stick

⅔ cup (95 grams) dark chocolate,
   broken into pieces

Granulated white sugar

Freshly grated nutmeg

1. In a medium saucepan over medium-low heat, add the milk, vanilla pod, and cinnamon stick and cook until the mixture boils.

2. Remove the pan from the heat and add the chocolate pieces, stirring until the chocolate melts completely.

3. Whisk the hot chocolate vigorously until it froths on top and add sugar to taste.

4. Dust with nutmeg and serve with perhaps just one (more) pastry.

# LONDON STEAMED PRAWNS

"We had brought pâté en croûte with us and French bread
and large red prawns."

—MICHAEL ROGERS, *Endless Night*, 1967

### ❦ SERVES 2 ❦

Published the day before Halloween in Britain and America, this novel reads as spooky and dark as the holiday it preceded. The title comes from William Blake's poem "Auguries of Innocence," but Christie reportedly took inspiration for the story from a tale told by her daughter's first mother-in-law. The mystery revolves around Gipsy's Acre, land that by legend belongs to gypsies (an old, occasionally pejorative term for the Romani people, who originated in the Rajasthan region of India and migrated by way of Persia to Europe). Despite warnings that outsiders aren't welcome, a gifted architect builds a home on this land for Michael Rogers and his new wife, Ellie, an American heiress. When they receive a telegram that the house is finished, Michael and Ellie travel from London, bringing wine and a celebratory picnic. The food doesn't fit the rural English atmosphere, nor does Ellie, a foreigner, or the beautiful new house. Generally larger than shrimp, prawns have ten legs, including three pairs of claws. Shrimp, which come in more varieties, also have ten legs but only one pair with claws. At this time, coastal communities routinely eat prawns, cheap and plentiful, but inland and in Europe, they prove harder to obtain, making them a prized, status ingredient. At Gipsy's Acre, the newlyweds would have enjoyed them cold, after steaming.

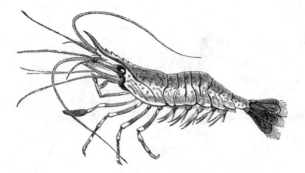

¼ teaspoon sea salt

1 pound (450 grams) prawns, shells on

Seafood seasoning (optional)

Lemon wedges (optional)

Cocktail Sauce (page 57) (optional)

1. In a large pot (that fits a steamer basket) over high heat, add 4 cups (1 litre) of water and bring to a boil. Make sure the water level falls low enough that the steamer basket won't sit under water. Add the salt.

2. Dust the prawns with seasoning, if using, and place them in the steamer basket.

3. Carefully place the basket over the boiling water and steam until the prawns turn pink throughout, about 3 minutes.

4. Serve hot or cold on a platter with lemon wedges and/or Cocktail Sauce if desired and pair with a bottle of Sauvignon Blanc.

# MRS. MACDONALD'S SALMON CREAM

"Mrs. MacDonald's recipe for Salmon Cream. . . . Given to me as a special favour. Take 2 pounds of middle cut of salmon, 1 pint of Jersey cream, a wineglass of brandy and a fresh cucumber."

—TOMMY BERESFORD, *By the Pricking of My Thumbs*, 1968

### ⚜ SERVES 4 ⚜

Unlike Poirot and Miss Marple, Tommy and Tuppence Beresford have aged naturally from their debut in *The Secret Adversary* (1922). In that first adventure, young Tuppence Cowley fancied expensive dining at luxury hotels, such as the Savoy or Ritz. But now she accepts a tin of questionable sandwich paste for a meal rather than waste it, and Tommy, distracted, burns a chicken dinner. Christie deftly indicates the passage of time with this shift in values. In this story, the Beresfords have just retired, and the relevance of food involves the mystery of Mrs. MacDonald's Salmon Cream. In a secret drawer of a desk left to Tommy by his recently deceased Aunt Ada, he finds three envelopes. One contains five £1 notes; one contains an accusation of murder; and one contains this recipe. Jersey cream, double thick and rich, comes from cows bred on Jersey in the English Channel. If you can't lay hands on a pint, substitute with half a pint of whipping cream and another of sour cream.

1 medium cucumber

1 shallot

4 ounces (120 millilitres) brandy

1 teaspoon fresh dill

1 pint (470 millilitres) Jersey cream

2¼ pounds (1 kilogram) center-cut salmon

Sea salt

---

1. Peel the cucumber, remove the seeds, and grate the flesh. Drain and press between paper towels to remove as much liquid as possible.

2. Finely chop the shallot.

3. Mix the prepared vegetables with 1 ounce (30 millilitres) of brandy and the fresh dill.

4. Fold the vegetable mixture into the cream. Refrigerate until ready to serve.

5. In a medium glass baking dish, pour the remaining 3 ounces (90 millilitres) of brandy.

6. Place the salmon, flesh side down, in the baking dish, cover, and refrigerate for 2 hours.

7. Preheat the oven to 375°F (190°C).

8. Line a baking sheet with foil. Transfer the salmon to the baking sheet, skin side down.

9. Roast until the fish looks opaque in the center, approximately 12 minutes per 1 inch (2.5 centimetres) of thickness.

10. Place the salmon on a serving dish. Season with sea salt to taste; top, while still warm, with the cream mixture; and pair with a bottle of Pinot Noir.

# JACK-O-LANTERN DEVILED EGGS

"Supper went well. Rich iced cakes, savouries, prawns, cheese and nut confections. The eleven-pluses stuffed themselves."

—from *Hallowe'en Party*, 1969

### ❧ YIELDS 18 ❧

Halloween—the eve, or night, before the feast day of All Saints, or "Hallows"—has deep roots in the British Isles. It emerged more than 2,000 years ago from Samhain, a Celtic harvest festival halfway between the autumn equinox and winter solstice in which Gaels donned animal pelts, built bonfires, made sacrifices, and told one another's fortunes. The Romans conquered Britannia, as they called it, by A.D. 43, which paved the way for Christianity to reach the province. By the 800s, churches here were venerating Christian martyrs on November 1. The Protestant Reformation swept away many of the old celebrations, but the descendants of the Gaels, particularly in Ireland, brought the tradition to America, where it grew in popularity before igniting once more in 20th-century England with decorations and games inspired by the original festival. Rowena Drake's party features carved pumpkins, costume competitions, fortune-telling, bobbing for apples, and murder. After the games and some awkward dancing, the teens enjoy a spread of holiday-themed treats. Since the 1940s, deviling has evolved, with more mustard replacing the cayenne pepper and mayonnaise for the butter. This dish offers a welcome savoury option for any Halloween gathering.

9 large eggs

⅓ cup (75 grams) mayonnaise

1 teaspoon dry mustard

½ teaspoon Worcestershire sauce

Salt and pepper

1 teaspoon orange food colouring

½ teaspoon black food colouring

1 medium green onion

Pumpkin leaves or fall leaves for garnish (optional)

1. In a large pot, cover the eggs with water by 1 inch (2.5 centimetres).

2. Place the pot over medium-high heat and bring to a boil.

3. Leave the eggs in a rolling boil for 10 minutes.

4. Carefully remove the eggs from the pot and place in a large bowl containing 4 cups (1 litre) cold water and ice. Let the eggs sit for 20 minutes.

5. Peel the eggs and cut them in half lengthwise. Separate the yolks from the whites. Rinse the whites and set aside.

6. Mash the yolks and add 3 tablespoons mayonnaise, the dry mustard, Worcestershire sauce, and salt and pepper to taste. Mix with orange food colouring and blend until smooth.

7. Fill each egg white with the yolk mixture by spoon, pastry piping bag, or plastic freezer bag with a corner snipped off.

8. Mix the remaining tablespoon of mayonnaise with the black food colouring and decorate each egg with a jack-o'-lantern face.

9. Cut the green onion into small pieces and place at the top of each egg half as a pumpkin stem.

10. Transfer the jack-o'-lantern eggs to a platter decorated with pumpkin leaves or fall leaves.

1970s

A FTER the upswing of the previous decade, the 1970s brought new tumult to Britain. The oil crisis fueled record unemployment; inflation and taxation skyrocketed; and strikes paralyzed the country. While making strides for civil and women's rights, the kingdom also faced numerous terrorist attacks.

Many families had to sell old homes and estates or convert them to multiple-family homes or institutions, but everyone was having dinner parties. Foreign dishes, such as chicken tikka masala, paella, and spaghetti Bolognese joined the more traditional fare of ploughman's lunch, pork pies, and Scotch eggs. Wine, once the exclusive domain of the upper classes, became popular.

In this new world, Christie maintained her popularity and wrote a best-seller every year with a "Christie for Christmas." Hollywood adapted *Murder on the* Orient Express and *Death on the Nile* for the silver screen, and in 1974 *The Mousetrap* moved to the St. Martin's Theatre, where it still runs today.

By now Christie had reached her 80s. But rather than training a discerning eye on the latest changes in society, as in prior decades, her last novels center on remembrances of times past and lingering injustices. In *Elephants Can Remember*, Poirot and Mrs. Oliver talk to many voices from the past to sort out what happened years ago. *Postern of Fate*, the last Tommy and Tuppence novel, features old toys, old secrets, and a very old garden shed. *Nemesis* and *Sleeping Murder*, the last Marple stories, also explore unsolved crimes from the past, with the sleuth recalling many favourite treats and tastes.

As with *Sleeping Murder*, Christie wrote *Curtain*, the final Poirot novel, during World War II. In 1974, she suffered a heart attack and a serious fall, rendering her unable to write. Perhaps sensing the end, her daughter, Rosalind Hicks, authorized the retrieval of the *Curtain* manuscript from a bank vault and its publication at the end of 1975. The mystery returns to the past, but the past has become the present. Styles, the manor house setting of her first novel, has become a collection of apartments and rooms for rent. Here Poirot and Hastings solve their final murder case.

Agatha Christie died on January 12, 1976, age 85, at Winterbrook House, her home in Wallingford, Oxfordshire. She was buried nearby at St. Mary's Church in Cholsey. At her death, she ranked as the best-selling novelist of all time, a distinction she retains to this day. *The Mousetrap* also remains the world's longest-running play.

# BAVARIAN
# LEMON SORBET

"Food came. A vast boar's head pickled in aspic, venison, a cool refreshing lemon sorbet, a magnificent edifice of pastry—a super *millefeuille* that seemed of unbelievable confectionery richness."

—from *Passenger to Frankfurt*, 1970

### ❧ YIELDS 2 CUPS (0.5 LITRE) ❧

In Christie's final thriller, Sir Stafford Nye, a bored British diplomat, falls into a web of international intrigue that includes world domination and the return of Nazis. Suspects include a German countess, the daughter of an earl, the wife of the American ambassador, a pocket Venus (an old expression for a small, beautiful woman), an elder statesman, security operatives, and a secret organization. Undercover, Nye travels to the mountains of Bavaria, where the Countess von Waldsausen—perhaps the master criminal—hosts a banquet. Seated in a grand carved chair upholstered in gold brocade and decorated with gold fittings, the gräfin, wearing a tiara of precious stones and stiff orange satin, presides over a spectacular feast, which includes this refreshing dish that food historians have traced as far back as 3000 B.C. Ancient Asian cultures mixed crushed ice with various flavourings. Ancient Egyptians mixed ice with fruit juices, and in A.D. 37 Emperor Nero reportedly sent a slave into the mountains to collect snow for sweetening with honey and fruit juices. Many places lay claim to this delicious treat, but its modern roots lie in Italy, where, by the 1600s, vendors in every piazza sold crushed ice mixed with fruit.

*continues*

**3–4 large lemons**                    **1 cup (200 grams) granulated white sugar**

---

1.  Zest 1 of the lemons and juice all of them for roughly 2 tablespoons of zest and 1 cup (240 millilitres) of lemon juice.

2.  In a small saucepan over medium heat, combine 1 cup (240 millilitres) of water and the sugar. Stir until the sugar dissolves completely. Remove from the heat and allow to cool.

3.  Stir the lemon juice and zest into the cooled syrup, pour the mixture into a freezer-safe bowl or metal loaf pan, and place in the freezer.

4.  Every 30 minutes, remove the sorbet from the freezer and stir with a fork. Repeat until the sorbet freezes light and fluffy.

# SEPTEMBER
# ROAST PARTRIDGE

"It is very difficult to get partridges nowadays, and they're
very expensive. I should enjoy a partridge—a whole partridge—to
myself, very much."

—JANE MARPLE, *Nemesis,* 1971

## ❧ SERVES 1 ❧

In this reflective novel, the final Marple story that Christie wrote, a recently
deceased wealthy friend of the frail sleuth asks her to solve an unspecified crime
from the distant past. Jason Rafiel, whom Marple met at the Golden Palm Hotel
on St. Honoré in *A Caribbean Mystery,* has proposed that, if she does, she can
earn £20,000. He arranges a bus tour and introductions to certain people. She
must do the rest. The story begins with Miss Marple imagining the delicacies
she'll enjoy with the money: roast partridge and a box of marrons glacés. Miss
Marple's choice of meal has meaningful layers. In the waning years of the Victorian era and the Edwardian decade, shooting parties gathered on the first day
of September, and, for the next week or two, the whole village feasted on the
wild birds. This dish from her own treasured past celebrates solving a mystery
from her friend's troubled past. The English partridge, a small bird, feeds just
one person, and she doesn't intend to share it.

1 small partridge, roughly
   1¼ pounds (0.5 kilogram)
1 tablespoon olive oil
Salt

½ tablespoon fresh chopped thyme
Ground black pepper

*continues*

1. Preheat the oven to 350°F (180°C).

2. Rinse the partridge under cool running water, pat dry with paper towels, and coat with the olive oil and salt to taste.

3. Place the seasoned bird in a small casserole dish. Pour 1 cup (240 millilitres) of water into the dish and add the thyme and some pepper to the water.

4. Loosely cover the partridge with aluminum foil, leaving space between the foil and the bird, and roast for 30 minutes.

5. Remove the foil and baste the bird with the cooking juice from the casserole dish.

6. Roast, uncovered, for 30–35 more minutes.

7. Remove the partridge from the oven and let it rest for 5 minutes before serving.

8. Pair with a small glass of Sherry and a box of marrons glacés.

# LITERARY LUNCHEON MERINGUES

"Mrs. Oliver arrived at the last course of the grand luncheon with a sigh of satisfaction as she toyed with the remains of the meringue on her plate. She was particularly fond of meringues and it was a delicious last course in a very delicious luncheon."

—from *Elephants Can Remember*, 1972

### ❧ YIELDS 24 ❧

In the chronologically final novel to feature both Poirot and Mrs. Oliver, Christie revisits her feelings about literary luncheons. Mrs. Oliver always declines invitations to them: "What a mistake for an author to emerge from her secret fastness," said the fictitious crime writer in *Mrs. McGinty's Dead*. But this time Mrs. Oliver does go, enjoying the speakers, her luncheon companion, and the food very much—especially these French meringues.

*continues*

**4 large eggs, room temperature**

**1 pinch fine salt**

**1 cup (200 grams) superfine (caster) sugar**

**½ teaspoon vanilla extract**

---

1. Preheat the oven to 250°F (120°C).

2. Line 2 baking sheets with parchment paper.

3. Carefully separate the egg whites from the yolks.

4. With a stand mixer fitted with a medium bowl and a whisk attachment, whisk together the egg whites and salt on medium-high speed until soft peaks form.

5. Gradually add the sugar, 1 tablespoon at a time, while continuing to whisk. Continue until all the sugar has dissolved.

6. Add in the vanilla extract and whisk on high for 3–5 more minutes, until the mixture stiffens.

7. Spoon a heaping tablespoon of the meringue mixture on the lined baking sheets. Repeat with the rest of the mixture.

8. Decrease the heat to 200°F (90°C) and bake the meringues for 1 hour 30 minutes.

9. Turn the oven off and leave the meringues inside it overnight, or at least 8 hours, to cool completely.

10. Store them in an airtight tin for up to 1 week.

# KITCHEN GARDEN CASSEROLE

"This is a casserole. Smells rather good, don't you think? I put some rather unusual things in it this time. There were some herbs in the garden, at least I hope they were herbs."

—TUPPENCE BERESFORD, *Postern of Fate*, 1973

## ❧ SERVES 6 ❧

The last novel that Christie wrote is the final Tommy and Tuppence Beresford adventure, and food has helped develop their full character arc. Some 50 years ago, Tuppence craved only the finer things in life, including food served at luxury hotels. During and just after World War II, rationing made meals a bland and boring challenge. Just a decade ago, Tuppence barely paid any attention to preparing meals or what Albert, first their assistant and then butler, had prepared. Now she's cooking from a kitchen garden. Christie occasionally mixed foxglove with edible herbs as a method of murder, but Tommy Beresford happily avoided that fate here.

1 pound (450 grams) potatoes

¾ pound (400 grams) turnips

1 large leek

½ head small green cabbage

1 pound (450 grams) sausages

3–4 tablespoons unsalted butter, room temperature, plus more for greasing

3 teaspoons fresh chopped thyme

2 teaspoons fresh chopped sage

Salt and pepper

1 cup (240 millilitres) vegetable or beef stock

*continues*

1. Thinly slice the potatoes; peel and thinly slice the turnips; trim and thinly slice the leek; thinly shred the cabbage; and slice the sausages diagonally ½-inch thick.

2. Preheat the oven to 375°F (190°C).

3. Grease a 9-by-13-inch (22-by-33-centimetre) casserole dish with butter.

4. Reserving enough potato slices for the top, layer the casserole dish with the potatoes, then turnips, then leeks, and then cabbage.

5. Layer the sausages atop the vegetables and season with thyme, sage, salt, and pepper.

6. Repeat the layering process, seasoning the meat each time, until you use all the prepared ingredients. Place the final layer of potatoes atop the uncooked casserole.

7. Slowly pour the broth into the dish, letting the liquid penetrate the layers.

8. Cover and bake for 45 minutes.

9. Remove the lid and dot the top of the casserole with small bits of butter.

10. Reduce the heat to 325°F (190°C), return the casserole to the oven, and cook it, uncovered, for 20 more minutes.

11. Pair with a hearty white wine, such as a white Bordeaux.

# GINGERBREAD LOAF

"'They had a very good cook—she gave me a wonderful recipe for baked apple pudding—and also, I think, for gingerbread. I often wonder what became of her.'

'I expect you mean Edith Pagett, madam. She's still in Dillmouth. She's in service now—at Windrush Lodge.'"

—JANE MARPLE AND THE DRAPER'S ASSISTANT,
*Sleeping Murder*, 1976

### ❧ YIELDS 1 LOAF ❧

Christie wrote the first draft of this mystery prior to 1944, when it takes place. In it, Miss Marple comes to the aid of a young woman who has odd reactions and visions in the house that she has just purchased. For example, she sees a man quoting *The Duchess of Malfi*—a 17th-century tragedy in which a man strangles his sister—while strangling a blond woman named Helen. Miss Marple determines to help this young woman uncover the past, refusing to allow a sleeping murder to lie unsolved, and of course Christie uses food to showcase Marple's craftiness. The sleuth strategically visits wool and fabric shops with older saleswomen eager to chat, mentions two recipes for baked goods, and lulls a target into revealing the whereabouts of a possible witness to past events. Miss Marple located Edith Pagett at Windrush Lodge, acquiring the clue she was seeking and a gingerbread recipe, which you can enjoy with custard or lemon curd.

*continues*

2 cups (240 grams) bleached all-purpose (white) flour

½ teaspoon salt

¾ teaspoon baking soda

1½ teaspoons ground ginger

1 teaspoon ground cinnamon

⅓ cup (75 grams) unsalted butter, softened, plus more for greasing

⅓ cup (65 grams) lightly packed brown sugar

1 large egg

¾ cup (180 millilitres) light molasses

¾ cup (180 millilitres) buttermilk

---

1. Preheat the oven to 350°F (190°C).

2. In a large bowl, mix together the flour, salt, baking soda, ginger, and cinnamon.

3. With a stand or hand mixer set to medium speed, cream the butter, brown sugar, egg, and molasses.

4. Add ⅓ of the dry mixture into the creamed mixture, then roughly ⅓ of the buttermilk. Repeat 3 times.

5. Grease a loaf pan and pour the batter into the pan.

6. Bake for 40–45 minutes, until the cake springs back when lightly touched.

7. Let it cool for 5 minutes and remove from the pan.

# ANOTHER PERFECT CUP OF COFFEE

"The aroma of coffee came to our noses—a delicious smell. The coffee at Styles was an uninteresting muddy fluid, so we all looked forward to Mrs. Franklin's brew with freshly ground berries."

—ARTHUR HASTINGS, *Curtain*, 1975

### SERVES 2

After Christie's heart attack and fall in 1974, her daughter, Rosalind Hicks, withdrew the manuscript for this novel from safekeeping in a bank vault and arranged for its publication. In the story, written during World War II, Christie reunites Poirot with Hastings—for the first time since *Dumb Witness* (1937)—at the same country house as her first published work, making this the second mysterious affair at Styles. As in that novel, houseguests meet after dinner for coffee, and murder ensues. So this collection ends as it began: with a cup of coffee. The world of coffee had changed a great deal since 1920 and the percolated pot served by Emily Inglethorpe to family and guests. Invented in Italy, automatic espresso machines fanned out across cafés and restaurants around the world in the 1930s. That same decade also saw the development of instant coffee, created by the Swiss to handle a boom crop in Brazil. Coffee drinkers quickly accepted the freeze-dried powder, and coffee became a shelf-stable staple in every household. By the 1970s, when this mystery finally appeared, faster, more efficient automatic-drip coffeemakers were replacing the old percolators in most homes. At the same time, the tradition of fresh roasted coffee was re-emerging. Cafés selling freshly brewed coffee made from freshly roasted beans became common in every village and town.

*continues*

From a local roaster, buy the freshest, best beans packaged in a vacuum-sealed bag. Keep the beans fresh not by storing them in the refrigerator or freezer but in an airtight container at room temperature. Always grind your own beans: coarse for a French press, medium for an automatic machine or pour-over, and fine for an espresso machine. Use filtered water or bottled spring water and dioxin-free filters or a reusable filter. Use the hot water 30 seconds after a full boil, never use the hot plate of a coffee machine, and never reheat the coffee. Thoroughly clean your coffeemaker at least once every three months.

**4 heaping tablespoons of coffee beans of choice for 4 tablespoons of grounds**

1. Set a kettle filled with 2 cups (500 millilitres) of filtered water over high heat to boil.

2. While waiting for the water to boil, in a coffee grinder, grind the beans to a medium grind, about 30 seconds, depending on the grinder.

3. Place a coffee filter over a small coffee pot and add the grounds to the center of the filter. Gently tap them to create an even surface.

4. When the water boils, remove the kettle from the heat and let it sit for 30 seconds.

5. Pour 1 ounce (30 millilitres) of hot water on the grounds and wait 30 more seconds.

6. Pour half of the remaining water in and let it sit for another 30 seconds.

7. Slowly pour the remaining water into the filter.

8. Enjoy 2 perfect cups of coffee in Poirot's memory.

# GAS MARK
# CONVERSION TABLE

| CELSIUS | GAS MARK | FAHRENHEIT |
|---------|----------|------------|
| 110°C | ¼ | 225°F |
| 120°C | ½ | 250°F |
| 135°C | 1 | 275°F |
| 150°C | 2 | 300°F |
| 165°C | 3 | 325°F |
| 180°C | 4 | 350°F |
| 190°C | 5 | 375°F |
| 205°C | 6 | 400°F |
| 220°C | 7 | 425°F |
| 230°C | 8 | 450°F |
| 245°C | 9 | 475°F |
| 260°C | 10 | 500°F |

# DISHES BY MEAL

# DINNER

# DESSERT

# BEVERAGES

# MENUS

## BREAKFAST WITH THE BANTRYS

An Englishman doesn't always have time for the full breakfast described in *Dead Man's Folly*. When at home with no guests, Arthur and Dolly Bantry might enjoy this simple meal.

**A Perfect Cup of Coffee**
from *The Mysterious Affair at Styles* (page 3)

**Orange Marmalade from Gossington Hall**
**served with toast**
from *The Body in the Library* (page 75)

**Poached Eggs at Chimneys**
from *The Secret of Chimneys* (page 12)

# LUNCH WITH ARIADNE OLIVER

Mrs. Oliver abhors a literary luncheon. She dislikes meeting people and, worse, she might have to talk about writing. But she does love a good lunch like this with a friend.

**Moroccan Mint Tea**
from *Destination Unknown* (page 112)

**Whole Chicken Soup**
from *After the Funeral* (page 106)

**Regatta Lobster Newburg**
from *Peril at End House* (page 31)

**Little Castle Puddings**
from *The Mystery of the Blue Train* (page 19)

Miss Marple likes to try new foods on holiday, such as the passion fruit she had for breakfast in the Caribbean. But for teatime in England, she prefers her sandwiches with the crusts off and, a childhood favourite, seed cake.

**A Perfect Cup of Tea**
from *The Moving Finger* (page 79)

**Crab and Salmon Sandwiches**
from *Sad Cypress* (page 67)

**Old English Seed Cake**
from *At Bertram's Hotel* (page 137)

**Gingerbread Loaf**
from *Sleeping Murder* (page 159)

# DINNER WITH POIROT AND HASTINGS

Poirot and Hastings often eat out together at one of the detective's favourite restaurants, where he is well known to the chef and the other regulars. Occasionally, they eat at Poirot's flat in Whitehaven Mansions where Poirot himself or Georges will create a delicious meal such as this. Pair with a bottle of red Bordeaux.

**A Perfect Omelette**
from *Mrs. McGinty's Dead* (page 102)

**Grilled Steak Frites**
from *Dumb Witness* (page 52)

**Soho Baba au Rhum**
from *Lord Edgware Dies* (page 33)

# SUNDAY DINNER WITH THE BERESFORDS

In Christie's day, many English households enjoyed a joint roast for Sunday dinner. To stay authentic to period, make the Sunday Roast Leg of Lamb (page 000). Tommy and Tuppence Beresford, however, may do it a little differently. Pair with a bottle of Chardonnay.

**Mrs. MacDonald's Salmon Cream**
from *By the Pricking of My Thumbs* (page 144)

**Kitchen Garden Casserole**
from *Postern of Fate* (page 157)

**Pêche Melba**
from *The Secret Adversary* (page 5)

# HALLOWEEN MURDER MYSTERY

A murder took place at Rowena Drake's Halloween party, but this menu should accompany a fictional murder mystery. No one need die for chocolate cake.

**Jolly Roger Cocktail**
from *Evil under the Sun* (page 71)

**Jack-o'-Lantern Deviled Eggs**
from *Hallowe'en Party* (page 146)

**September Roast Partridge**
from *Nemesis* (page 153)

**Devon Boiled Potatoes**
from *And Then There Were None* (page 62)

**Another Delicious Death by Cake**
from *A Murder Is Announced* (page 97)

# CHRISTIE FOR CHRISTMAS

In England, it's not all turkey, sprouts, parsnips, and mash for Christmas. Many wonderful dishes appear on the table during the holidays. A Christmas tribute to Christie should include regional treats, gastronomic treasures, and, of course, cream—neat or in the form of Sherry.

**Lucy Eyelesbarrow's Mushroom Soup**
from *4.50 from Paddington* (page 120)

**Christmas Eve Lobster Soufflé**
from *Hercule Poirot's Christmas* (page 58)

**Sunday Roast Leg of Lamb**
from *The Big Four* (page 17)

**Welsh Cakes**
from *Why Didn't They Ask Evans?* (page 39)

This sweet and savoury spread will delight any fan and make it a meeting to remember.

**Hollywood Daiquiri**
from *The Mirror Crack'd from Side to Side* (page 131)

**Oysters Rockefeller on the *Orient Express***
from *Murder on the* Orient Express (page 36)

**Canapés Diane**
from *Three Act Tragedy* (page 42)

**Chelsea Banana and Bacon Sandwich**
**quartered and served with maple syrup**
from *The Pale Horse* (page 129)

**Meadowbank Marvel**
from *Cat among the Pigeons* (page 124)

**British Coffee Cake**
from *The Sittaford Mystery* (page 29)

**Tiger Nut Sweets**
from *Death Comes as the End* (page 83)

**Drug Store Coffee Ice Cream Soda**
from *The Man in the Brown Suit* (page 10)

**Lemon Squash on the *Karnak***
from *Death on the Nile* (page 54)

# APPENDIX: PUBLICATION HISTORY

*The Mysterious Affair at Styles* published by John Lane, New York City, in 1920 and The Bodley Head, London, in 1921

*The Secret Adversary* published by The Bodley Head, London, and Dodd, Mead & Co., New York City, in 1922

*The Murder on the Links* published by The Bodley Head, London, and Dodd, Mead & Co., New York City, in 1923

*The Man in the Brown Suit* published by The Bodley Head, London, and Dodd, Mead & Co., New York City, in 1924

*The Secret of Chimneys* published by The Bodley Head, London, and Dodd, Mead & Co., New York City, in 1925

*The Murder of Roger Ackroyd* published by William Collins & Sons, London, and Dodd, Mead & Co., New York City, in 1926

*The Big Four* published by William Collins & Sons, London, and Dodd, Mead & Co., New York City, in 1927

*The Mystery of the Blue Train* published by William Collins & Sons, London, and Dodd, Mead & Co., New York City, in 1928

*The Seven Dials Mystery* published by William Collins & Sons, London, and Dodd, Mead & Co., New York City, in 1929

*The Murder at the Vicarage* published by Collins Crime Club, London, and Dodd, Mead & Co., New York City, in 1930

*The Sittaford Mystery* published by Collins Crime Club, London, and as *The Murder at Hazelmoor* by Dodd, Mead & Co., New York City, in 1931

*Peril at End House* published by Collins Crime Club, London, and Dodd, Mead & Co., New York City, in 1932

*Lord Edgware Dies* published by Collins Crime Club, London, and as *Thirteen at Dinner* by Dodd, Mead & Co., New York City, in 1933

*Murder on the* Orient Express published by Collins Crime Club, London, and as *Murder in the Calais Coach* by Dodd, Mead & Co., New York City, in 1934

*Why Didn't They Ask Evans?* published by Collins Crime Club, London, in 1934 and as *The Boomerang Clue* by Dodd, Mead & Co., New York City, in 1935

*Three Act Tragedy* published as *Murder in Three Acts* by Dodd, Mead & Co., New York City, in 1934 and by Collins Crime Club, London, in 1935

*Death in the Clouds* published by Collins Crime Club, London, and as *Death in the Air* by Dodd, Mead & Co., New York City, in 1935

*The A.B.C. Murders* published by Collins Crime Club, London, and Dodd, Mead & Co., New York City, in 1936

*Murder in Mesopotamia* published by Collins Crime Club, London, and Dodd, Mead & Co., New York City, in 1936

*Cards on the Table* published by Collins Crime Club, London, in 1936 and by Dodd, Mead & Co., New York City, in 1937

*Dumb Witness* published by Collins Crime Club, London, and as *Poirot Loses a Client* by Dodd, Mead & Co., New York City, in 1937

*Death on the Nile* published by Collins Crime Club, London, in 1937 and by Dodd, Mead & Co., New York City, in 1938

*Appointment with Death* published by Collins Crime Club, London, and Dodd, Mead & Co., New York City, in 1938

*Hercule Poirot's Christmas* published by Collins Crime Club, London, in 1938; as *Murder for Christmas* by Dodd, Mead & Co., New York City, in 1939; and as *A Holiday for Murder* by Avon Books, New York City, in 1947

*Murder Is Easy* published by Collins Crime Club, London, and Dodd, Mead & Co., New York City, in 1939

*And Then There Were None* published as *Ten Little Niggers* by Collins Crime Club, London, in 1939; as *And Then There Were None* by Dodd, Mead & Co., New York City, in 1940; and as *Ten Little Indians* by Pocket Books, New York City, in 1964

*Sad Cypress* published by Collins Crime Club, London, and Dodd, Mead & Co., New York City, in 1940

*One, Two, Buckle My Shoe* published by Collins Crime Club, London, in 1940; as *The Patriotic Murders* by Dodd, Mead & Co., New York City, in 1941; and as *An Overdose of Death* by Dell Books, New York City, in 1953

*Evil under the Sun* published by Collins Crime Club, London, and Dodd, Mead & Co., New York City, in 1941

*N or M?* published by Collins Crime Club, London, and Dodd, Mead & Co., New York City, in 1941

*The Body in the Library* published by Collins Crime Club, London, and Dodd, Mead & Co., New York City, in 1942

*Five Little Pigs* published by Collins Crime Club, London, and as *Murder in Retrospect* by Dodd, Mead & Co., New York City, in 1942

*The Moving Finger* published by Dodd, Mead & Co., New York City, in 1942 and by Collins Crime Club, London, in 1943

*Towards Zero* published by Collins Crime Club, London, and Dodd, Mead & Co., New York City, in 1944

*Death Comes as the End* published by Dodd, Mead & Co., New York City, in 1944 and by Collins Crime Club, London, in 1945

*Sparkling Cyanide* published by Collins Crime Club, London, and as *Remembered Death* by Dodd, Mead & Co., New York City, in 1945

*The Hollow* published by Collins Crime Club, London, and Dodd, Mead & Co., New York City, in 1946

*Taken at the Flood* published by Collins Crime Club, London, and as *There Is a Tide...* by Dodd, Mead & Co., New York City, in 1948

*Crooked House* published by Collins Crime Club, London, and Dodd, Mead & Co., New York City, in 1949

*A Murder Is Announced* published by Collins Crime Club, London, and Dodd, Mead & Co., New York City, in 1950

*They Came to Baghdad* published by Collins Crime Club, London, and Dodd, Mead & Co., New York City, in 1951

*Mrs. McGinty's Dead* published by Collins Crime Club, London, and Dodd, Mead & Co., New York City, in 1952

*They Do It with Mirrors* published by Collins Crime Club, London, and as *Murder with Mirrors* by Dodd, Mead & Co., New York City, in 1952

*After the Funeral* published by Collins Crime Club, London, and as *Funerals Are Fatal* by Dodd, Mead & Co., New York City, in 1953

*A Pocket Full of Rye* published by Collins Crime Club, London, in 1953 and by Dodd, Mead & Co., New York City, in 1954

*Destination Unknown* published by Collins Crime Club, London, in 1954; serialized as *Destination X* by the *Chicago Tribune* in 1955; and published as *So Many Steps to Death* by Dodd, Mead & Co., New York City, in 1955

*Hickory Dickory Dock* published by Collins Crime Club, London, and as *Hickory Dickory Death* by Dodd, Mead & Co., New York City, in 1955

*Dead Man's Folly* published by Collins Crime Club, London, and Dodd, Mead & Co., New York City, in 1956

*4.50 from Paddington* published by Collins Crime Club, London, and as *What Mrs. McGillicuddy Saw!* by Dodd, Mead & Co., New York City, in 1957

*Ordeal by Innocence* published by Collins Crime Club, London, in 1958 and by Dodd, Mead & Co., New York City, in 1959

*Cat among the Pigeons* published by Collins Crime Club, London, in 1959 and by Dodd, Mead & Co., New York City, in 1960

*The Pale Horse* published by Collins Crime Club, London, in 1961 and by Dodd, Mead & Co., New York City, in 1962

*The Mirror Crack'd from Side to Side* published by Collins Crime Club, London, in 1962 and as *The Mirror Crack'd* by Dodd, Mead & Co., New York City, in 1963

*The Clocks* published by Collins Crime Club, London, in 1963 and by Dodd, Mead & Co., New York City, in 1964

*A Caribbean Mystery* published by Collins Crime Club, London, in 1964 and by Dodd, Mead & Co., New York City, in 1965

*At Bertram's Hotel* published by Collins Crime Club, London, 1965 and Dodd, Mead & Co., New York City, in 1966

*Third Girl* published by Collins Crime Club, London, in 1966 and by Dodd, Mead & Co., New York City, in 1967

*Endless Night* published by Collins Crime Club, London, in 1967 and by Dodd, Mead & Co., New York City, in 1968

*By the Pricking of My Thumbs* published by Collins Crime Club, London, and Dodd, Mead & Co., New York City, in 1968

*Hallowe'en Party* published by Collins Crime Club, London, and Dodd, Mead & Co., New York City, in 1969

*Passenger to Frankfurt* published by Collins Crime Club, London, and Dodd, Mead & Co., New York City, in 1970

*Nemesis* published by Collins Crime Club, London, and Dodd, Mead & Co., New York City, in 1971

*Elephants Can Remember* published by Collins Crime Club, London, and Dodd, Mead & Co., New York City, in 1972

*Postern of Fate* published by Collins Crime Club, London, and Dodd, Mead & Co., New York City, in 1973

*Sleeping Murder* published by Collins Crime Club, London, and Dodd, Mead & Co., New York City, in 1976

*Curtain* published by Collins Crime Club, London, and Dodd, Mead & Co., New York City, in 1975

# Acknowledgments

First, I must thank my grandmother who introduced me to Agatha Christie. As a curious ten-year-old, I found my grandmother's collection of paperbacks and fell in love, embarking on a lifetime of reading and rereading Christie and the fabulous adventure of writing this book.

So many people gave me their love and support as I completed this project. It cannot be overstated how much I owe the success of this book to their time, effort, and enthusiasm. Beginning with my daughter, Heather Pierce. She encouraged me from day one, edited initial drafts, and brainstormed evolutions of the book's structure with me to the final version. You wouldn't be reading this tome were it not for her. I thank Colborne Communications, specifically Greg Iannou and Paula Chiarcos, for their editorial support and expertise in the early days.

My next thank you goes to the three women who did a great deal of cooking, recipe revision, and taste-testing for me: Joanna Farrer, Jane Reid, and Lorraine Spragg. Their assistance and their taste buds proved invaluable. I couldn't have asked for better recipe collaborators.

A very big thank you to my family and friends for a lifetime of support. Some of you were cooking, and the rest of you were taste-testing (the good and the bad!). I am in your debt.

To Kathryn Willm at The Rights Factory, both for championing my idea and then for holding my hand as we readied the manuscript for the publisher. To James Jayo and all the others at Countryman Press, particularly Ann Treistman, Maya Goldfarb, Jess Murphy, Allison Chi, Devon Zahn, Devorah Backman, and Rhina Garcia. Thank you for helping me create and publish this very special book. You have my sincere gratitude. Without a doubt, I wouldn't be here without you.

All the acquaintances, colleagues, and total strangers who encouraged me to persevere, you will never know that sometimes only your kind words kept me going. I did it! Thank you all.

# INDEX